Praise for

Building the World's Greatest Hig. ....

the work upon which this book is based

"For educators and school leaders who long for a positive school culture, the numerous, time-saving, cost-effective methods of identifying and celebrating student success are found in this book."

–**Trevor Greene**, *2013 MetLife/NASSP National High School Principal of the Year*

"As a teacher at the World's Greatest High School, I know that these strategies will work for building strong school cultures and climates. 'Park' started our traditions twenty-two years ago with students, staff and community using these principles and we are still going strong."

–**Debi Weiss**, *Warren E. Shull Outstanding High School Activities Director by California Association of Directors of Activities, Activities Director – Ayala High School*

"I have had the privilege of knowing Richard Parkhouse for over 25 years. His passion for creating positive school cultures is second to none. When he's on your campus, lives change, and students and staff understand the vision while school pride can be seen and felt. His heart and passion are infectious."

–**Janet Roberts**, *CADA President, California Associate of Directors of Activities (2013), Activities Director – Chino Hills High School*

"School culture is the critical ingredient to a great high school. Richard has been in so many schools, his insights and stories inspire and encourage school leaders everywhere."

–**Phil Boyte**, *Learning For Living, School Climate Consultant and Educational Speaker*

"Richard Parkhouse is a thought leader in positively changing campus culture and climate. His insights and observations are 'spot on' and he continues to provide that next step in making our schools the places we all want them to be."

–**Patrick Maurer**, *Speaker and Educator*

"The lessons learned and inspiration gained from Richard Parkhouse lasted beyond my high school years at the World's Greatest High School. High expectations and no excuses push me today as I work in Baltimore City to organize and advocate for ALL children, regardless of race, neighborhood or socioeconomic background, to attend world-class schools. If you want to push yourself, your school or your community to excellence, meet the World's Greatest Mentor, Richard Parkhouse."

–**Shannen Coleman Siciliano**,
Former Student

"I have had the opportunity to work with Richard Parkhouse throughout the years and this book reflects his passion for uncovering unique strategies that help support student as well as adult learning. I think this book is a must read for any educator looking for affirmation on the impact of 'outside the box' thinking and leadership as well as examining student motivation from the inside out."

– **Keith M. Bell Sr.**,
Superintendent, Euclid City Schools, Euclid, Ohio

"Richard Parkhouse is a proven performer in helping schools build productive school culture! As a former high school principal, 'Park' helped us instill a caring school climate for all students!"

– **William F. Roberts IV**,
Assistant Superintendent, Hacienda La Puente Unified School District

Other Works by Richard Parkhouse

Building the World's Greatest High School

Visit Park's Website

www.edalchemy.com

Other Works by Dr. Guy E. White

Exiting The Bakesale® Fundraising Training

Building the World's Greatest High School

The First Seven Days: Exciting Step-By-Step Meetings

Get Free Training at Guy's Website

www.exitingthebakesale.com

Building the World's Greatest High School Workbook

The Official Companion Text

Richard Parkhouse & Dr. Guy E. White

World's Greatest High School™ is a trademark of EDalchemy, Inc. and is licensed by EDalchemy, Inc. to Richard Parkhouse, Guy E. White and Triumphant Heart International, Inc.

Published in collaboration between:

Triumphant Heart International, Inc.
12188 Central Ave., #366
Chino, CA 91710

EDalchemy, Inc.
20687-2 Amar Road, #231
Walnut, CA 91789

Get free training at www.worldsgreatesthighschool.com

Library of Congress Control Number: 2013951963

wghs_wb1_131122

Dedication

To those that swallow the red pill and daringly stretch to become their World's Greatest each day

Table of Contents

Note from the Authors

As the title implies, this is a companion text. Though you will find value in the activities without the master-text Building the World's Greatest High School, *it is highly recommended that you have it, read it, and consult it in tandem with this workbook.*

Want to go deeper? Want to further impact your instruction, students, and school? Visit our website and sign up for more free training:

www.WorldsGreatestHighSchool.com

Foreword

with our dear friend, Valerie Vera-Mineer

I love my job! I love the start of a new day and the opportunity to connect with my students and staffulty. This is my twenty-second year of teaching and I feel like a first year teacher. Many changes have occurred in my life over the years – some good and some not so good: lessons learned, wisdom gained, new ways of looking at people and at the world. I feel like a newly hatched butterfly, ready to spread my wings and fly! I am in a good place, embracing my divorced status and enjoying being single. I love the journey of raising two incredible thirteen-year-old teenagers and marveling at their skills and talents. They open my eyes to witness life from a male teenage perspective. I am blessed being surrounded by family and friends who support me, accept me, and, still, challenge me.

One group of people who challenge me, inspire me, and with whom I have a heart-to-heart connection includes incredible individuals who have a passion for education and see that, daily, we have the opportunity to "change lives and impact futures." One man who is a member of this group is Richard Parkhouse. I call him "mentor." I call him "friend." Richard Parkhouse, along with Dr. Guy White (another member of this incredible group) wrote a book that has truly changed the way I think, the way that I look at my role as an educator, and the way I see myself. I am renewed!

In reading *Building the World's Greatest High School*, I realized that the book was not just about high school, but about EVERY school. I teach at a junior high school in Southern California with over forty fellow educators and about twelve hundred students.   We have a wonderful school; I teach in a positive learning environment, a safe campus, where students and staffulty are engaged. Parents are highly visible and involved in supporting the learning of their child. But this book made me think "is there more we could do?" The answer was a resounding "YES!"

As one of two leadership teachers on my campus, I lead the portion of our student leadership program concerned with student recognition. After reading Park and Guy's book, we knew we wanted this idea to be the school-wide thematic direction for the fall of 2013. We had our student leadership classes read the book over the summer as their recommended reading. When we gathered in August for our five-day Leadership Camp, we knew they had the foundation to build the World's Greatest JUNIOR High!

Let the creativity begin! We had a construction theme during Leadership Camp. We carried this theme into the first days of the school year. Student leaders and staffulty wore yellow plastic construction hats on the first day of school. The school was decorated in yellow and black colors. Banners and posters were made with statements such as "Building Begins Now," "If You Build It, They Will Come," "Caution Coyotes [our mascot] At Work," to name a few, along with the six World's Greatest Values listed in the book. Our front entrance states on a poster, "Through These Gates Walk the World's Greatest." Our student leaders and staffulty were highly visible, in their construction hats, to assist students to their new classes and welcome these Coyotes to the World's Greatest Junior High! Electricity was in the air! Students and staffulty made comments about how great it felt to be back on campus! To top off the day, we gave away "Honor Pops," a play on the brand name of a well-known iced fruit snack, to everyone on campus at lunch. It was a welcomed treat on the sweltering first day of school.

The second day of school was just as important as the first to make an impact on our student body. We had a mini rally to kick off this year's theme of "Building the World's Greatest Junior High!" The staffulty proudly wore our new shirts with the words "Coyote Construction," which displayed a coyote drilling on a construction sign. (Shout-out for Dan Van Beek at T-Graphics West for designing and donating the shirts.) During our mini rally we shared with our students the differences between "No Hope," "Mediocre School," and "World's Greatest" schools. We briefly explained the six World's Greatest Values shared in the book. To connect the students with the philosophy of the book, we had each student write on an index card his or her gifts, talents, and skills. On another index card each wrote his or her personal goal for the year. We have taken those cards and have them displayed on two separate bulletin boards for the entire school to see. We also display the staffulty index cards with the same information. The staffulty are the foundation on which the students stand to build the World's Greatest Junior High. We invited the local newspapers to capture this theme. The response to and viral nature of the World's Greatest Values is like nothing we have experienced at our school.

This fall, I asked my junior high student leaders, "What was the one thing that you learned from the book?" The big themes I heard were:

1. Don't forget the Kileys and Alyssas. Assist them. When students help other students transform, massive growth follows for all.

2. The only way to start helping others is to first step out of my own comfort zone and build relationships with my peers.

3. Regardless of a student's GPA, all students have needs that we can meet as leaders.

4. There are many different types of talents; you just need the right eyes to see them.

5. Leaders place themselves in the vulnerable position of having their hearts invested – even if it could end in heartbreak.

6. Bad life circumstances outside of school do not always doom students to failure; sometimes it's the reason they persevere.

When asking myself the same question, three things come to mind: The first thing I learned from *Building the World's Greatest High School* was the value of "All Kids Have Futures." I agree with the notion that I am not merely teaching my subject area, but I am, indeed, teaching my students to become better human beings. It is through our daily interaction that we can learn from each other. I have to admit that I have, for most of my career, kept my students' desks in rows. This year with the influence of this book and changes in our national vision of education with Common Core State Standards implementation, I have my desks in groups of four. I gave each student a leadership survey the first week of school to see how they defined themselves. The survey is color coded so that each student learns the color of their leadership that indicates their strengths. Using this survey, I placed one student with one color in each group. This way, the students would have the opportunity to work with people who have different strengths than their own. I love this new arrangement. Students often share with one another and discuss their work with each other for clarity, reassurance, and understanding. Not only is curriculum discussed, but newsworthy events as well (I ask them to check the daily news to find out what is going on in the world; I do teach World History!). Sometimes we just share what they did over the weekend. The opportunity to engage and connect with the group along with the entire class is available. I also can walk around the entire room and interact with the small groups and individual students. Everyone is asked to participate daily. It is wonderful to see my Kileys, Alyssas, and Austins all working together, learning, and strengthening each other. I believe this is working for us.

The second thing I learned from the book was the value that "No One Gets Anywhere Without a Teacher." Each person has a most inspirational teacher who made an impact in his or her life. Most often this teacher assisted him or her to become a better human being. Reading this in the book was a nice reminder that my students would not be the same without me. Now, I also know that I would not be the same without them. One of the best things about our profession is that we have the opportunity to meet so many students in one year. In that year, we can learn so much from each other. The student-teacher relationship is reciprocal. We never really know what impact we make on our students at the time, but it is such a gift when students return and let you know that you made a difference in their lives!

Finally, thinking about the book, the most significant value that impacted me was "Everyday is The Opportunity to Become The World's Greatest Me." Timing is everything. When I first read the book, I didn't get through it all. I wasn't ready to listen and learn. The second time I read the book, I attacked it like I did back in college, highlighting and taking notes as I read. "A happier, more wholly developed you will not only be a better, happier teacher, but a better, happier human being as well." Yes, I believe this wholeheartedly! You cannot give away that which you don't have. The more balanced I am intellectually, physically, emotionally, and spiritually the more I can offer in my relationships in the classroom as well as at home. I desire to live an authentic life.

As you can see, this book has made an impact. The beautiful thing about this journey is I don't know where it is going to take me, where it is going to take us, where it will make a change in the lives of my school family. As the book says, "At The World's Greatest High School, each person on campus seeks to become a better version of 'me' than the day before – and its members work purposefully to develop each person's gifts, talents, and skills." My job as an educator is my calling. I am ready to become the World's Greatest Me. I can be the change agent: the match, the spark, and the flame. I have the desire to become a better human being, so I can assist my students (and my children) in doing the same. Great teachers provoke action and inspiration in their students.

I am ready for this challenge, this opportunity for growth. Won't you join me in becoming the World's Greatest You? If not me, who? If not now, when?

Leave a legacy!

Valerie Vera-Mineer

World History Teacher

Junior High Student Leadership Advisor

Mother of Max and Myles ☺

Want to hear more about how Valerie and other educators like her implemented what they learned in Building the World's Greatest High School? *Visit our website and sign up for more free training:*

---

www.WorldsGreatestHighSchool.com

Introduction

"School transformation requires personal transformation. The World's Greatest Educator works each day to personally transform into a better version of himself or herself."

Wow! A workbook! When Park and I sat down by a pool in Lake Havasu a few springs ago, we were like two sorcerers putting all the magic we had learned into a single cauldron for the first time. When two educators are exchanging ideas about which they are passionate, magic happens: sparks fly, ideas join, and something new is created. Some have likened this merging of ideas to a third mind in the room. What emerged from those initial days in the desert is what became *Building the World's Greatest High School*. However, after the book was published in March of 2013, what happened next was unexpected: more people joined in our third mind, as educators began implementing the World's Greatest Values throughout the nation. Within weeks of educators reading the book as near as the school down the street from my house in Southern California, and as far away (at least that we know of) as Finland, we began receiving requests for two distinct types of "next steps": deeper activities, questions, and dares for (1) the solitary educator who is improving his or her personal teaching practice and school, and (2) whole staffs who want to implement the World's Greatest Values school-wide. This workbook delivers upon all of those requests! If you find yourself in one or both of the above categories, this workbook is for you.

Just as the excitement and contributions of others began to intermix with our hopes for our continuing contribution to schools, we also noticed where school families needed to go deeper with their World's Greatest work and did not know how to do that. Consider specifically: How are you reaching out to the individual Kileys and Alyssas at your school? With so much already happening on your campus to assist students who need extra support, how are you INDIVIDUALLY reaching out to these students to help them be one day better than the day before? How do these students know that they are INDIVIDUALLY seen, recognized, and appreciated on your campus by a myriad of school family members? These are the types of questions that are addressed in this workbook, to enable educators like you to become better masters of teaching practice and to enable YOU to assist others to do the same. Toward this goal, this workbook will show you how to lead yourself, your students, and your staffulty through life-changing activities, questions, and dares.

www.worldsgreatesthighschool.com   7

Of great importance is the way that you work with the Austins at your school – the advanced students. Ironically, it could be said that the focus on serving "all students" has, at times, led to forgetting those students who seem to need the least help. All too often, students who are "at the top" academically are celebrated for their pencil-driven accolades yet are largely ignored elsewhere on campus. All too often, students who are not "in crisis" (at least by the school's measure) yet are not in the top ten percent of student achievers find themselves as unknowns. These Austins need your attention as well. They need your individualized recognition of their contributions to your school family. These Austins contribute through the arts, activities, athletics, and, yes, academics. Are you enabling these school family members to be more fully seen? This workbook will not just assist you in enabling these students to be leaders and change agents inside and outside your campus gates. This workbook will also expand your ability to see the needs of these Austins – the needs that are often ignored.

On your campus today, there is a deeply entrenched system of "haves" and "have-nots." This system impacts the way that educators work with students inside and outside their classroom. This system affects the way that your student leaders approach their work with their whole school family. It even affects the way that administrators organize and structure staff meetings. This system largely decides who gets a voice, who gets suspended, who gets financial resources, and who gets the bulk of your attention as a change agent at your school. Many of the activities of this workbook will show you where these haves and have-nots exist on your campus. Further, we'll show you how to seek out and enable contributions from all. Best of all, we'll assist you in having the eyes to see the amazing gifts that all students, staffulty, parents, and community partners are *already* providing to your school.

Take a moment to read this paragraph at the opening of this workbook: You are one of the determined educators who takes the time, energy, and steps required to deepen your teaching practice. With all the responsibility that you are holding, by reading this workbook, you are signaling your willingness to take on more. When you engage in activities that focus on your personal development and transformation, you expand your ability to see and do. The wonderful consequence of this type of transformation is that others join in with you. You are not a singular radical particle in the ecosystem of your school; you are an integral part of everything that happens every day (even if you don't quite see or understand that). As you work through this book, know that all that you do is not just on behalf of yourself; your work is on the behalf of every life connected to you inside and outside your school. Cheers.

All Kids Have Futures

Chapter 1

"Work with your inner game and outer game."

You are a male tenth-grade student with a 1.0 GPA ("D-" average). It's the first day of school. You swagger through the hallways with your best new t-shirt, depicting a scantily clad woman, and your nearly empty backpack. It's time for math class. You failed the last two years of math. This is your third time taking remedial algebra. As you enter the classroom, you see your classmates. If you averaged the GPAs in the room, the number would be around 0.8 ("F" average). Many of you have taken this class before. The bell rings. The teacher begins by reading the rules of his class: the late work policy, the dress code policy, the grading policy, how to tear your paper from the spiral binder, and what beverages are permitted and which are not. There's no connection between you, this room, this subject matter, or this educator; each feels separate, unmotivated/unmotivating, and, frankly, a bit hopeless. As things stand, nothing will change – and you know it. What do you do? Do you sit and do the work? Is it easier to do nothing at all? To be honest, besides the teacher (depending on his mood) and, occasionally, your academic counselor, will anyone really notice if you just do nothing much at all? You might think, "Things are as they are, and they'll probably always stay that way."

How do you reach students such as these? Think about the ways in which your school has already attempted to assist these students. Chances are, if you are like any of the hundreds of schools into which Park and I have collectively stepped, you have probably had many staff meetings discussing how to reach the (labeled) "unmotivated" student. In our observation, what is often discussed is what we dub "external interventions." These are the things that we do "outside" of students (and outside ourselves) to change their behavior. We change their schedules. We place them in special programs and courses. We group them. We have meetings with them and their support systems. We remediate them. We have them "assessed." We do lots of things around and outside of struggling students, but rarely do we delve inward into the most important place of focus regarding these students. Rarely do we look into the way in which we personally "see" these students. Rarely do we own up to our behaviors as educators that result from our way of seeing students we deem to be struggling. What do we believe about these students? How does that way of seeing these students impact the way we go about working with them?

Imagine having a son or daughter who is not performing well in school in terms of GPA. They are not going to graduate if things continue as they are. They are placed in a special program that requires them to attend an intervention period during the school day where they receive special instruction about math and language arts. One evening, attending Back To School Night, you hear your child's intervention teacher commenting in the hallway to another teacher, "Well, I have lots of students in my intervention class who don't want to learn; many CAN'T learn! That's why they are in my class!" Hearing the candid words of this educator, would you feel comfortable leaving your child in such a class? Would you not want to transfer your kid immediately? When an educator does not believe that success is possible, how effective can he or she be at impacting struggling students for the better? These are the kind of "internal" questions that need to be addressed along with the external discussions about student interventions.

Because you are reading this, we'd like to think that you believe that any student's success is possible, regardless of their past. We hope that you believe that all students want to have good, happy lives – though the particulars of each student's dream are different from another's. However, you know from observation that each and every educator brings the lens of his or her life experience into the classroom. This lens carries with it a way of seeing all students, including struggling ones, and greatly impacts the way in which an educator goes about working with such students. We need to examine the way we see our students. We need to start with our own way of seeing and working with our students, because, in the end, regardless of how students are grouped, scheduled, classified, remediated, or disciplined, we are the people looking them in the eye in our classroom. We are the ones working hand-in-hand with them. If I cannot clearly see my students, because my lens is carrying strong judgments like "this student can't learn" or "he is a troublemaker," then how can I truly do my greatest work with these students? As is, I will always be limited by one thing that I truly CAN control: my way of seeing and working with students.

When we say that the most fundamental principle in teaching is "all kids have futures," we must start by looking at our "inner game" first and expand to look at our "outer game" next. We challenge you to continue the outer game discussions and interventions at your school as you take some time to look within yourself and at your way of seeing and working with your students. You may be surprised by what you find. We challenge you to make these discussions part of the community fabric of your school. When we can take our lens of life off, put it on the table, and examine it with others, we can begin seeing what our habitual tendencies offer us and how they hinder us; then, we can make changes to more impactfully reach all our students.

Reflection Questions

1. To what degree does everyone at your school have the conditions for growth and life? What's missing?

2. To what degree does your school act in all things as if "all kids have futures"? Where does the school fall short?

3. What is one example of how your school acts like all kids DON'T have futures?

4. What is one example of how your school acts like all kids have futures?

5. How would your classroom(s) be different if you believed that all kids have futures?

Deeper Considerations

Two years after marrying, I decided that it was time to seriously start working on building my body. I had three university degrees under my belt already; my mind was feeling pretty accomplished. However, looking in the mirror each morning, I felt like there was a serious disconnect between the growth I had internally experienced and the outer shell that was lugging that experience around town. In the city center where I lived, there was a martial arts studio that embodied all that I was looking for: incorporating multiple disciplines in which to work, like martial arts, acrobatics, yoga; having dedicated instructors who had been working with a lineage of teachers for decades; and, most importantly, aligning me with a teacher who would challenge me as an individual. So, with much excitement, I purchased the required uniform, made a payment, signed a release, and began my first class.

Three minutes into the first day, I was in hell. I was panting, sweating profusely, and already getting dizzy. Each request by the teacher became more and more foreign to me; I thought he was crazy. "Jump over this bag?" I said to myself, "WHY?" "Run sideways? Who does that?" "Why are we doing pushups upside down with my feet up the wall?" Needless to say, I was challenged in a way that I never had been before. This teacher was not prescribing an entire workout program to twelve people; he was individually selecting exercises for each of us. All of us were working as hard as I was – even the people who had been in this class for years. When my mind and body calmed down and as the feeling returned to my face, I felt this immense sense of community: we were all there working as hard as we could, in the ways that were individually hardest for us. We were each working with our "edges," pushing our limits just enough to feel the great challenge, but not so much that we broke under the pressure. Every single one of us returned the next day to class, because all of us wanted to be pushed to that limit again. We could make progress because someone was showing us those edges.

When we talk about you working with your inner game, we are talking about you pushing up against your edges, feeling uncomfortable, and expanding your ability to be more tenderhearted toward students and their potentials. You can get at those edges and grow by experiencing the discomfort, anger, frustration, or any other emotional brick that gets lobbed against your skull during your work with students. This is not a "feel good" experience; this is a "when am I getting my buttons pushed?" kind of experience. These experiences can point exactly to where we are being invited to expand, hearten, and grow. The hardest part is allowing oneself to experience the pain and make the conscious decision to stay emotionally in the room.

Deeper Questions

1. When do you find yourself feeling the most discomfort (sad, angry, tired, uncomfortable, frustrated, etc.) with students during the workday?

2. Describe a specific moment with one student wherein you felt this discomfort. What were the specifics? Who was it? When? What were they doing? What were you doing? (Choose an everyday moment, not an exceptional situation.)

3. As plainly as you can say it, in what specific behavior was the student engaging that was causing you discomfort?

4. Personally, what do you believe about this behavior?

5. What does this belief offer you? Your students?

6. In what ways does this belief close out certain students? Close you down?

We Dare You

As this is the first dare, allow us to give you a behind-the-scenes preview of what these dares will offer through the course of this workbook. Each day, we come to campus and do many of the same things (with slight variations) that we did every day prior. This does not mean you're boring; it means you are human. Naturally, we tend toward that which is more comfortable, predictable, and consistent. We know what hallways we avoid on the way to our classrooms because of foot traffic. We know what time we need to leave our houses to get to our schools on time. We have spots in which we prefer to sit during staff meetings. We have favorite (or at least unconsciously preferred) places to stand or sit in our classrooms. Needless to say, there is much that we do by routine. The bell has already trained many of us. Accordingly, the purpose of these dares is to mess with the routine way that you see and go about your day.

What will that offer you? By changing the angle from which you see your world just a bit, you can begin to break from the routine, defy No Hope or Mediocre High School, and step into a better version of yourself each day. As a great mentor used to say to me, "When nothing changes, nothing changes." These dares will guide you to something that Park and I would like you to see in the course of your work in building your World's Greatest High School. Further, when you "see" the thing that we are pointing out, we'll suggest an action for you to take accordingly. For many reading this, it will be very uncomfortable to take these dares. We encourage you to muster your bravery, your personal aspirations, and your hopes for your students. You are doing these dares on their behalf.

This first dare is all about examining the way that you see your students. Over the course of the next week, you will have ten opportunities (two per day) to exercise this dare. We encourage you to keep these pages tabbed or bookmarked so that you can refer back to them each day. Try not to think about this dare in terms of "Is it working or changing me?" or "Did I do it right?" or "Is my school better now?" Instead, as best as you can, think of each experience, each time you exercise the dare, as a precious gem that you pick up off the floor and dust off. This gem was there the whole time, but you took the moments required to see that it was sitting right there, completely unnoticed. It's through the gathering of these little gems that over time you acquire the sight to see your World's Greatest High School and the strong ability to build it. So, with that, it's time to go gather some gems.

The Dare

Each day, for the next ten days, notice instances in your classroom where you are experiencing discomfort because of specific student's actions or attitude. This discomfort may be anger, irritation, fatigue, physical pain, or any other similar sensation.

Twice each day, during such moments, <u>in your mind</u>:

1. Name the student who is causing you discomfort;

2. Name the specific behavior that is eliciting discomfort in you;

3. Name the emotional feeling that you are experiencing as a result.

In your mind, you might say, "Tim, throwing sunflower seeds on floor, anger." Similarly, you could say to yourself, "Marta, sharpening pencil with teeth, deep concern."

Finally, now that you have mentally touched that emotional feeling, to the best of your ability, simply allow it to float away. You might, as a sign of this, decide to take a deep breath and let out a big exhale.

Daily Questions

Take a few minutes to answer the following questions about your experience. We recommend that you keep your notes for this dare in a separate journal or notebook.

1. What were these emotional feelings attempting to communicate to you today? What were they saying about students? About you?

2. What did you want to offer this student? Did that feel less possible because of his or her actions?

3. Despite his or her actions, what could you have still offered this student, but did not?

Want to go deeper? Want to further impact your instruction, students, and school? Visit our website and sign up for more free training:

www.WorldsGreatestHighSchool.com

Three Types of Schools

Chapter 2

"Are you saying that we are No Hope High School?"

Since naming the three types of schools, we have largely encountered two types of educators. First, there are the educators who hold those around them most responsible for making the school what it is in terms of "No Hope," "Mediocre" or "World's Greatest." These educators believe that they have made every reasonable attempt (at least in what they see as their sphere of influence) to make the school a better place. They are proud of what they have accomplished – but they don't always feel that way about their colleagues. Second, there are those educators who exceedingly hold themselves, personally responsible and are practically willing to bear the "sins" of the entire school upon their shoulders. "If I could have just done one thing better," they say, "one more student could have 'made it.'" Which one are you?

There's a lesson in taking responsibility for your actions on both sides of this dichotomy. When you feel that you have done your best but others have not, you carry a narrow view of how others approach their work with students. Labels quickly appear and you build a mental map of "dos" the "don'ts" on your campus. You thicken the boundary between you and the other people teaching in your halls, all because you have such a firm belief in what you are doing and what they are not doing. Conversely, if you are the one willing to take the responsibility for the "whole show," like so many administrators and activities directors are willing to do, you are shortchanging yourself, minimizing the great things that you have done, and failing to see how others are not rising to the sacred task put before them (to nurture kids). There's a balance between nurturing a tender heart for others and cultivating a tender heart toward yourself.

The labels "No Hope" and "Mediocre High" are not ones that you put up on the marquee of your heart to use to start the blame game or to label yourself into better behavior. Instead, they are guideposts – invitations to something more open, life giving, and befitting you (as a teaching professional) and your students. These labels are not permanent, or fixed, or ones that apply to the whole of your school. Take responsibility for your actions with the same spirit of nurturing gentleness in which you approach your teaching. You would never bring a stick to your classroom to maintain discipline, so stop emotionally beating yourself and beating others to make

www.worldsgreatesthighschool.com   17

the school a better place. Don't work against "No Hope" or "Mediocre High." Instead, take that feeling of "No Hope" or "Mediocre High" and let that be the force you work *with* to make your school a better place. Let that feeling of hurt, disappointment, anger, boredom, stuckness, etc. be the indicator of what is needing attention – the kind of attention you give someone who's sick and needing an expert physician.

Each day, you walk to class most likely utilizing the same route as every other day. You "know" your hallway. You "know" your classroom. You "know" your students. Yet if one thing is off, if one thing is out of place, if one thing goes wrong, you feel the smack of reality hitting that image of what you *think* is those hallways, classrooms, or students. When our mental image does not match our reality, we freeze, we get angry, we resist. What would it be like to take those feelings and utilize them to make our school a better place?

Many of us don't like to go to doctors, because they get into the details of our health – the uncomfortable places that we'd rather not look. They weigh us and take our blood pressure when we arrive. They look into our mouths and ears. They listen to our heart. They ask us the question, "What brought you into the office?" – the answer to which is rarely roses and candy. The physician provides her assessment and advice. We have a choice: (1) heed her words and change, or (2) resist and do little or nothing.

If you slowly walked your campus each day for ten minutes, choosing a different route each time, breathing deeply and keeping your eyes open and curious to what was around you; if you listened to what the voices around you were saying and the tones with which the words were being said; if you smelled the air, the car exhaust, the wind through the planters, and the 104-degree heat wafting through backpacks and shirts; and if you truly tasted that cafeteria food that you eat when you forget to bring your lunch to school, you would "hear" the assessment and advice that your heart may be bringing forward for you and your school. Sometimes, all you'll have is an emotion to guide you forward; but what will you do with it?

At that moment, you have a choice: (1) heed the pull to something greater, or (2) resist the feelings and fall back into habitual patterns. We can take responsibility for our actions in our school without beating up ourselves. We can take responsibility for our actions in our school without beating up others. Instead, we can wake up more and more each day with a fresh view of what is going on in our hallways and classrooms. We can wake up to what is happening in our hearts and let that be the way we start true transformation on our campus. Will you dare to hear your heart? Each day, we can become better than the day before.

Reflection Questions

1. Which of the three types of schools do you think most closely matches yours?

2. What are the qualities of your school that make you say that?

3. How is your school already successful in being like the World's Greatest High School?

4. What is ONE area in which your school needs improvement?

Deeper Considerations

We educators have an interesting relationship with "school improvement." When we are in staff meetings talking about making our school a better place, we often get angry, frustrated, or bored at the plethora of "new ideas" being paraded in front of us (perhaps that's how you found out about *Building the World's Greatest High School*). We want things to "change," but strangely, when things do change we feel uncomfortable. There is a clear pull between (1) what we want to happen for our school, and (2) our habitual, daily patterns. We want our school to change but often get frustrated when the change does not go the way we expected or wanted. We have a comfortable way of going about our lives. When people disrupt that way of life, we get very protective. So, the paradox is: for the school to improve, we all have to get uncomfortable and be willing to stay uncomfortable.

The seemingly sad secret that a dear mentor whispered to me once in a staff meeting reminds me of this paradox. She had taught for much of her adult life and was near retirement. She had seen nearly every change imaginable in the school system from the early 1960's to that moment. That morning, as the principal was discussing the newest program to solve our problems, my mentor's lines of wisdom on her face curled up into a smile as she leaned in and whispered to me, "Guy, there is no magic arrival. You will be improving your teaching until the day you leave the classroom. Even then, your students will still be hunting you down for advice." As a first year teacher, that shocked me: "I am *never* going to arrive? There is *no* finish line?" As I have grown in this way of life (teaching), I have consistently found that every day I am still improving as a teacher. Every moment with every student offers the chance to be kicked off my throne of experience and be surprised. Every day, I am uncomfortable and incomplete. Because I am more and more open to being uncomfortable, I am more and more open to becoming my World's Greatest Me.

If you're anything like me, when faced with difficulty, it's much easier to detour around your own classroom and focus on what others are doing on your campus. I could spend my time focusing on the deficiencies in the front office, in the activities office, in the athletics office, on the lawn in front of the school, or on the traffic that blocked me this morning from my favorite parking spot. I could call my students "lazy" or "unmotivated." What would it be like to realize you were experiencing discomfort in your world and, instead of heading to the hills to avoid the feeling or blaming the feeling on others, grab that feeling by the hand, sit down with it for coffee, look it in the eye, and say, "[Anger, Disappointment, Fear, etc.], what are you trying to tell me about my work with my students and school family today?"

Deeper Questions

1. To what degree can you "arrive" as an educator? When does improvement as an educator slow down or cease?

2. Explain how your answer to the above question impacts your work with students now. In the future?

3. Name one emotion that you experienced today during your work with students, parents, or fellow staff. Describe the situation in which this feeling arose.

4. What was that emotion communicating to you? To what was that emotion pointing that needed/needs attention?

5. Ultimately, if that emotion was your friend, giving YOU loving advice, what would it be saying about or asking of YOU?

We Dare You

As mentioned above, we have a comfortable set of habits in which we engage each day. One of the most common habits that educators engage in each day is the route that they take to and from their classrooms. For example, if you were to draw a map of your movements on your school campus each day for the next year, you'd most likely see a set of dark lines leading to two or three locations, utilizing the same route each time. On this map, there may be a few errant lines leading out into the less traveled areas. Further, there would be entire areas that you never step into at all during the year. What happens there?

Interestingly enough, when we have interviewed educators, we have found that, even on their most traveled routes to and from their classrooms each day, most educators have little or no knowledge of WHOM they pass in the hallway each day. They may be able to describe a handful of students, but of the dozens of people they pass, only a few catch their eye. In the pursuit of making ourselves, our students, and our schools better, could we be missing something important in the hallways around us each day?

Consider the fisherman who boards his boat each day and goes to a certain spot to fish. He walks across the dock, gets on his ship, looks to the horizon, and use his GPS to find his way out to that favored fishing ground. He catches a few fish each day – not as many as he wishes. In fact, he is a bit pissed off that he makes this trek every day, getting up very early in the morning, preparing the best bait possible, only to drop his line in the water and be disappointed by the regular small catch. "Don't these fish know this is the best bait around? I must be surrounded by some pretty disturbed fish for them not to want to take a hold of this hook! What mediocre fish!" Some nights, the fisherman thinks he should move to a whole new ocean altogether to fish there. "If I was in *such-and-such* ocean, these fish would act totally different." One day, on the way to his boat to make that long trek out into the water, he slips on the dock and falls flat on his face. He feels the ache of his head as he comes to his senses and as his vision returns from a blur. To his surprise, just as his eyes focus, he looks off the dock near where his boat is parked each day to see the water is teeming with excited, eager, hungry fish. The fish he was looking for were there *every* day – it's just that he had never slowed down enough from his routine to see them there.

Sometimes, what we are seeking is only a few steps away – all we have to do is take those steps with eyes open. This dare will open your eyes to your school family in a new way.

The Dare

Each day for the next ten days, notice when you are walking to or from your classroom at the start of the day, during a passing period, during lunch, or after school.

Twice each day, choose to make a switch in your routine path and do the following:

1. Detour from your pre-planned route entirely. Walk the opposite direction if you must. Yep, you can still head to your destination – just take a different route than usual or planned.

2. Walk slower (perhaps ¾ the usual speed).

3. As you are walking, keep your eyes open and forward. Make eye contact with those who pass you by. Look at the people who surround you to your left, right, and front. Do you see new faces? Do you see some old ones?

4. Acknowledge others through eye contact, a head nod, a wave, or a kind word. Acknowledge slightly more people than feels comfortable to you.

After you get to your destination, you may return by any route you please. This dare has been completed.

Daily Questions

1. To what extent was it difficult to step out of the norm of your day and see / acknowledge others?

2. To what extent were others engaged with one another? What evidence was telling you that?

3. Based upon what you saw today (and previous days you did this dare), what patterns need to be disrupted within your school family? What patterns did you see that should be encouraged?

Want to go deeper? Want to further impact your instruction, students, and school? Visit our website and sign up for more free training:

www.WorldsGreatestHighSchool.com

The World's Greatest Values

Chapter 3

"We need to move from the 'How' to the 'Why.'"

Park and I have this crazy idea that there is a reason we (educators) do what we do each day in the way that we do it. That is, there are both internal and external driving forces that make us decide to interact with our students in our fashion; to instruct students utilizing our chosen strategies; and to bring a certain emotion, energy, or spirit to our work (or lack thereof). External driving forces include the pressures placed upon us educators by the district, the county, and the state. They also include the way in which others (students, staffulty, parents, etc.) interact with us each day. When someone gives us lemons, we don't like it, and we might be showing our displeasure to others. In the edusphere, we have often observed a trend among professional developers, administrators, and teacher leaders to emphasize the external: "What are we *doing* as teachers and *how* are we doing it?"

There are many reasons to focus on the external. First, it's much easier (and the norm) to have these types of discussions with other educators. We can talk about what we see, what we do, how we do it, and how we can improve what we are doing. Second, "teaching" itself manifests as an external act, so talking about how we are teaching is a very natural way of improving instruction. Finally, the "what" and "how" conversation is the basis for deeper conversations that we can have about teaching. Without the definition and description of what we are doing in our classroom, there simply is no hope of analyzing our practice, comparing and contrasting it to our best practice or the practice of others, and creating new ways of teaching. Often, however, doesn't the conversation stop with the discussion of "what" and "how"? What about the "why"?

When I was about six years old, growing up in Chino, California, my father had a huge vegetable garden. It was about one third of an acre (pretty huge by most people's standards). He would grow every type of fruit and vegetable imaginable. We had just moved from a suburb outside of Los Angeles, and this "cow town" seemed to be out in the middle of nowhere to my brother and me. My dad was still wearing polyester slacks and shirt, a gold chain, and leather loafers as he would garden with a cigarette hanging out of his mouth; he would later graduate to a t-shirt, jeans, and boots. One summer, he had grown a huge patch of watermelons. They looked amazing. The outside husk was dark green with white marbling. These looked better than anything we could have found at the supermarket. After much anticipation, it was time to have our first taste. My mother, all 115 pounds of her, walked out to the field, squatted down, and braced herself to pick up this huge, heavy watermelon. As she lifted, at once, the watermelon levitated five feet in the air and she fell backwards to a huge splash of dust. That huge watermelon weighed nothing at all! After we all ran out into the field to dust her off and investigate, we found that a gopher had eaten the entire innards of the fruit. Worse yet, much of the beautiful watermelon patch had suffered the same fate. On the outside, everything looked healthy, juicy, and ripe for the picking. On the inside, there was little going on.

In our world as educators, we spend so much time focusing on the skin of the watermelon, looking for evidence of what is going on inside, that we forget that we can cut open that thing and "see" for ourselves what is internally happening. What is the inner game that is supporting the external actions that we take each day with our students? What is the inner world of our students doing to impact their way of learning in the classroom? What internal forces are shutting down their parents and preventing them from offering us the support that we seek as educational partners? Why do we do what we do?

We need to investigate and refine WHY we do what we do. An educator can put a banner up in our classroom and say, "This is the World's Greatest Classroom," but that does not make much sense if that educator's internal world is having him or her kick out students each morning who forget to bring their textbook to class, have failing students face away from the dry-erase board, or refuse to make eye contact with students altogether. How much can professional development about external content standards impact an educator who is depressed, angry, and taking it out on students each day? We need to look at the common core we share within our hearts on our campus. This way, our instruction can pour from that love and care that we nurture there.

In *Building the World's Greatest High School*, we presented to you what we (and a growing cadre of others) feel are the values of the most amazing schools on the planet. We have seen amazing transformations occur at schools where these internal values are discussed alongside external practice. When you talk about the "what" and talk about the "why" alongside one another, you crack open that shell around educators' hearts and get to that tender core that is at the root of their teaching. Before you can do that for others, though, you have to be willing to get to your own tender heart. That's what this whole chapter in this workbook is about.

Reflection Questions

1. What are one or two values in which you already believe? How do these values show in your teaching or work at your school?

2. What World's Greatest Values were "questionable" or ones about which you disagreed? Why?

3. Is there a value that you believe your entire school has already taken up and lives out each day?

www.worldsgreatesthighschool.com   27

Deeper Considerations

Educators love to show off their inner philosophy. When you visit school leadership trainings, conventions, and the like, you see lots of bracelet and t-shirt messages carried on people's bodies. Some educators have adopted stories that are meaningful to them and place buttons or pins on their lapels to show this. When you visit many classrooms, this same trend applies. When you look at many classroom walls, you'll find pithy statements of all kinds, often outwardly symbolizing the educational philosophy of the teacher. You might have such messages on your clothing, accessories, or walls. If you could design the perfect message to symbolize your belief(s) as an educator, what would this message say? Think about it.

In 2008, I was wearing lots of t-shirts and bracelets like the ones described above. In my student leadership class, I had posters everywhere touting philosophies of student and teacher leadership of all kinds. If you needed an inspirational message, I had a coffee mug for that. One day, my student leadership class and I were sitting in a circle talking about our hopes for our school. This was one of the most important activities that we would undertake each Friday – the day we set the heart agenda for the coming week. This week had been particularly hard for my students and me. Some new students had been transferred into my class without the usual student leadership application process and approval. Many of them, as they verbally stated, wanted nothing to do with student leadership. In our circle activity, a small group of these new students sat in one corner, talking amongst themselves. During the activity, when it was time for students to individually share their desires for their fellow students the coming week, these new students continued to talk amongst themselves quite rudely. Finally, I had enough of this and said, "Excuse me! Won't you join us in this conversation?"

Quite to my surprise, one of the students calmly looked into our circle and said, looking at us all, "You know, you all talk a lot about making students feel welcome in this school. You have lots of posters in this room about recognizing the unrecognized. You know, we," pointing to the other new students, "would love to feel as welcome here as you say you want to make everyone else feel on campus. Won't YOU join US?" I was floored.

Since that day, I know that there are really two outward messages that I carry: First, there is the message that I put on my clothes, bracelet, poster, or car bumper. This is what I WANT the world to see. Second, there is the message that I am showing through my actions. My hope: to make these messages as much the same as possible. When they say different things, I hope to have the courage to address that.

Deeper Questions

1. What outward message(s) do you, personally, display or state about your teaching or work with students? What do you want the world to see? What is the single word you would like to describe *you* as an educator?

2. What outward message(s) does your school display or state about its work with students, parents, and/or community? What does your school want the world to see?

3. To what degree do you live up to your message(s)? When do you do well? When do you do less well? Give specific examples.

4. To what degree does your school live up to its message(s)?

5. If you asked others, what do you think they would say is/are your message(s)? Personally? As a whole school?

We Dare You

This dare will launch you into the bulk of the transformation that will come from your work in this book. In short, this dare sets the stage for everything else. As best you can, DO NOT SKIP THIS.

Most of us are not the most objective judges of our own behavior. You have seen a photo of yourself shot at an inopportune instance: "Do I always look like that?" A student has seen you as you walked down the supermarket aisle in your Saturday casual clothes: "Does Dr. White always dress like an old man?" No one wants to see a video of him- or herself eating pizza. A "360-degree" evaluation is one of the most reliable ways to get a view of the entirety of a situation. If we rely solely upon our own evaluation, we are missing out on the greatest ways that we can grow.

Some readers will be uncomfortable regarding this dare, as it asks you to do something that many avoid in fear of what may result. Our humble request: dare to step into the discomfort, because that is where the growth happens. We ask our students to struggle with rigorous material each day so that they can advance. We too must be willing to step in and do the work. We do not grow in the absence of difficulty; we grow because of it.

Some readers may be tempted to let this dare be the end-all of this workbook. Consider: If you noticed a piece of gold sitting in a garbage can, you would not simply pick it up and walk away. You'd probably want to keep digging to see if there was more gold in there! Similarly, this dare will provide the means by which you can see where further digging is necessary. You'll find yourself astonished, disappointed, and motivated after completing this activity. Regardless, it's a starting point.

Before you embark on this dare, please complete this prework.

The Basics

1. Obtain from your records clerk a spreadsheet of all parent contacts for your entire school with phone numbers and home addresses.

2. Create a simple one-page survey (see next page). Distribute one survey to EVERY student on campus during the same period, on the same day. Have teachers collect completed surveys and submit to you. Offer a drawing/prize.

3. Distribute one survey via mail to EVERY parent connected to your campus. It's worth every penny. Have students return surveys to school. Offer a drawing/prize.

4. With your fellow staffulty, examine the results. What themes emerged?

The Dare

Create a simple survey utilizing the below questions as a guide. Keep it simple: no bubbles, no circled numbers. Keep the questions open so that you can get the open responses that will allow you to experience your students, parents, and school.

Survey

1. What are we doing well? What's the best thing about our school?

2. How could we improve?

3. How well do we treat students like "all students have futures"? Explain.

4. How could our teachers better serve our students?

5. What student gifts, talents, and skills do we ignore? What are we missing?

6. What is something we should start doing? Why?

7. What is something we should stop doing? Why?

Want to go deeper? Want to further impact your instruction, students, and school? Visit our website and sign up for more free training:

www.WorldsGreatestHighSchool.com

World's Greatest Expectations

Chapter 4

"Create a school where success is seen as the norm."

Think back to the dare in Chapter 2 of this workbook, when you deterred from your usual, planned route on your campus and walked into territory that you usually avoid or miss altogether. What strange sights were in this unusual land? What did you see on the walls? The ground? What smells lingered? What sounds peppered the air? Think about when you passed through these areas looking at the people who spent their time in this place; what do you think they were missing every day simply by taking THIS route instead of the myriad of others available to them? Most important, consider a specific area of campus through which you walked: If this were the only place that students spent time each day, what would this area alone teach your students about your school?

Physical spaces teach. When you visit the most famous amusement park on the planet, every detail of every space is painstakingly fashioned to induct you into the mindset (attitude) of this place. Consider the front gates of this place: they are filled with the noises of laughing children, joyful music, and the roar of the attractions within; they are infused with the smells of candy, fried confections, and sugary goodness; and they are lined with genuinely appreciative, smiling attendants, ready to take your ticket. You have the pass to the greatest place on Earth, and you just used it! From the moment you walk in, unless you are a generally unhappy person, you experience the rush of the possibility of the day: This could be your BEST day.

What do the front gates of your school teach? If you are like many of the schools into which we have walked, you probably have MANY entrances. Does your school have a sign that greets students? What does it say? Is there a triumphant arrival that is made possible through this gateway, or is it a pathway into boredom? Is it epic, or is it vanilla? You, your staff, and your students are DAILY inducted into your school in the sixty seconds it takes to get from the car to the front doors; what message of induction is sent by the front gates that greet them each day? Are you and your fellow "inductees" greeted by a sign that says "closed campus – trespassers will be prosecuted," or do the EPIC words "Such and Such High School – Home of the World's Greatest" meet you? Which would you prefer?

Consider your school's hallways. In my study of the leadership approaches of activities directors of highly successful high schools in Southern California, I discovered that "co-curricular" activities (often called "extracurricular" activities) are often defined as the activities in which students engage outside classrooms. This feels like a no-brainer, but think about that! This means that co-curricular activities don't simply happen in the gym, the field, or the multipurpose room. Co-curricular activities comprise all the time in between AND outside classes. The whiteboards of co-curricular activities, then, are the physical walls, floors, poster boards, and window spaces of the entire school. The instructional strategies of co-curricular activities are the movement of people through the halls, quads, etc.; the sensory experiences you purposefully infuse into the gathering of people; and the direct interactions that you facilitate between human beings. If the hallways, gym, fields, and social spaces of your school were a classroom, would the instructor be absent?

You have the power as a school to teach your students, staff, faculty, parents, community members, and trespassers alike that this school is the World's Greatest place for these students to be this morning to become the best versions of themselves they have ever seen. However, if you only attend to the classrooms within the boundaries of your entire campus, you are missing out on such a huge area of influence upon your school family. Simply highlight the non-classroom spaces on a paper map of your campus, and you'll most likely see that the non-classroom spaces of your school make up 50% or more of the entire "space" of your school. How are you utilizing this space as an interactive classroom for all?

When I was just starting out as a substitute teacher for various districts in Southern California, I stepped into some of the most decrepit, disgusting, ignored classrooms imaginable. Between the wet ceiling tiles, the coverless books, the desks filled with graffiti, and the carpets that had gum and God-knows-what stains on them, I often thought to myself, "Who allows such a place to be ignored like this such that THIS is the norm?" Frankly, we doubt there is a person reading this who thinks that such a classroom is excusable. We have laws about this sort of stuff! However, think about your own hallways; do you hold the same level of standards for the out-of-class teaching spaces on your campus that you do for the classroom? When you invest in utilizing the hallways, front entrance, gym, quads, restrooms, parking lots, etc. as a place where you can showcase that there are HIGH expectations for all at your school, ALL students have the opportunity to share in this common language of success. However, if you hide your school's budding "World's Greatest" culture solely within your classroom, that is a mediocre strategy at best. Invest in your out-of-classroom spaces. Take the movement beyond your classroom.

Reflection Questions

1. How will you show that you have high expectations for each person at your school?

2. How will you show everyone concerned that you actually mean "each person"?

3. What are some ways in which you can teach the people connected to your school that great things are expected for and from them?

4. What are some expectations that educators say they have about student behavior but don't actually mean?

5. What is one word that you want to define what is expected of students at your school? Do others believe in the same word? How do you know?

6. What actions would show that a student, staff member, or community member is fulfilling the expectation set by that one word? How do you know when an expectation has been fulfilled?

Deeper Considerations

There are many types of leadership that manifest within your local staff and faculty. You have worked, most likely, with people of all types of leadership style. You have worked with the transformational leader who inspires. You have worked with the wheeler-dealer who makes deals and trades to make things happen on campus. You have worked with those with little or no leadership capacity. Also, you have worked with one of the more troubling types of leaders: "leaders" who manage solely by exception – that is, their leadership only appears when a crisis or problem arises. This type of staff or faculty member is particularly troubling because they only respond to problems. They pose solutions only to silence and calm that which offends them or their sense of the rules. You probably have seen this quite often on your campus: teachers and administrators being irritated by a particular problem, like students wearing offensive t-shirts on campus, and responding for an intense number of weeks with detentions and other penalties. Beyond responding to the rules not being met, their leadership is relatively absent. These staff members appear most when they are troubled by something. Then, they disappear into their offices and classrooms until the next crisis arrives.

When you respond to crises alone, you find yourself in a perpetual state of disappointment. The flash point that springs you into action is only a result of seeing a problem. This is akin to visiting the same restaurant every day, knowing that every time you order you will be receiving the incorrect meal, guaranteed – yet you still keep going, yelling at the server for disappointing you, and being angry about the whole situation. What would it be like to step out from the role of "responder" into the role of "inspirer," "instructor," and "expert developer of human potential"? If you are reading this, we fervently believe that you largely have already made this shift. Will you help others take the leap, step in front of problems, and formulate a new way of life for those who walk your halls each day? Will you help your fellow educators stop focusing on putting out fires and, instead, find the source of the pains that your school family experiences?

To begin to transcend the suffering that your school experiences, you must, in part, get into the details of the daily experiences of your students, fellow educators, and community partners. Rather than responding solely to the loudest family members, you will need to carefully examine what each family member is experiencing (see Chapter 3 Dare) in his or her daily life. Then, consider what developmental steps must be undertaken by each person to make his or her life one step better each day. Finally, teach these developmental steps every day, everywhere. Teach them as if success was the norm.

Deeper Questions

1. Based upon the feedback you received in the Chapter 3 Dare, what daily experiences of students, staffulty, and parents deserve the most attention? Why?

2. Choose one of the daily experiences you listed above. Considering this daily experience, what is a single thing you will do each day to make students, staffulty, or parents one step better than the day before?

3. How will you take this developmental step for students, staffulty, or parents to a school-wide level? Inside classrooms? Outside classrooms?

4. What are some physical, tangible ways that anyone will be able to see that this developmental step is alive in your hallways? Posters? Art? Statues? Explain.

5. How will you be the leader assisting others in creating a transformation vs. the sole influencer or "doer" who stands alone?

We Dare You

The purpose of this dare is to allow you to be better able to ask for, hear, and respond to the feedback that your school community is giving you. In the following dare, you will make contact with past, present, and future students (or parents) and ask them targeted questions regarding their experience or anticipated experience as a student of your school. So often, when educators talk about making "data-based" decisions, they mean seeing through a very shallow, narrow set of data points about student performance (GPA, test scores, etc.). However, through the power of conversation, you can find out much more about the experiences of your students and what your school is yearning for. Before you making massive changes to the fabric of your school culture, see what "data" your school family can give you.

The Dare

This dare takes place in three phases. Complete every phase. This dare should take approximately three to seven days to complete.

Phase One (Past)

Utilizing the database wizardry of your front office administrative assistant or records office, obtain a list of the names, phone numbers, and GPAs of all students who graduated or exited from your school as seniors last year (if you are at a middle school, think of students who exited the eighth grade). Ask for the list to be organized by GPA, lowest to highest. Make contact with three previous students from each of the following GPA groups: (a) 0.0-0.5, (b) 0.6-0.9, (c) 1.0-1.9, (d) 2.0-2.4, (e) 2.5-2.9, (f) 3.0-3.6, (g) 3.7 and higher. Ask each previous student the following questions and write down their responses.

1. In what ways did we benefit you? Where did we wrong you?

2. Now that you have left our school, where are you today (work, school, etc.)? How did our school contribute to you getting there?

3. What could we have done to better help you to have the life that you want(ed) earlier?

Phase Two (Present)

Make contact with four current students at your school per GPA group. Attempt to get a member of each grade level in each GPA group (ninth to twelfth). Meet with four students at a time. In your "focus group" that you just created, ask these questions:

1. Is success the norm at our school? Explain. Why do you feel that way?

2. Who are we leaving behind? Explain. Why do you feel that way? Examples?

3. What do you think your future holds? How do you think the school is helping with that?

4. What makes this school a great place? What could we do better?

5. In what ways is the school not assisting you with your future? Examples?

As you are interviewing these students, act as if they are bearers of diamonds – they are!

Phase Three (Future)

Utilizing the same methods you employed in Phase One, gather the names of parents of students who will be joining your school NEXT YEAR. Interview two parents for each GPA group listed above. Ask them these questions:

1. What can our school do to make your student more successful?

2. What have other educators missed? What do you want us to see or do from the start?

3. Imagine it's four years from today, your student is a senior (or an eighth grader in two years if you are at a middle school), what do you hope your student will be able to say about his or her experience at this school?

If you have the opportunity, be open to the parents inviting their students onto the call with you.

Culminating Activity

Now that you have interviewed past, present, and future students (or their parents), examine what you have heard. For EACH question, write down all the themes of what was said in a text document. Adjust the size of the text for each theme depending on how often you heard that response. Make the text biggest for themes that appeared again and again. Make the text smallest for those themes that only appeared one or two times. Show these to your fellow educators.

When you are done, look at the sum of what you have uncovered. Consider: (1) What works well at this school? (2) Specifically, what needs to improve? (3) Who do you ignore, miss, or mistreat? (4) To what degree do you teach that success is the norm? (5) Based upon what you have discovered, what do you need to do FIRST?

Want to go deeper? Want to further impact your instruction, students, and school? Visit our website and sign up for more free training:

www.WorldsGreatestHighSchool.com

World's Greatest Mentors

Chapter 5

"No one gets anywhere without a Mentor."

Behind my desk sits a framed picture of Steve Jobs and Steve Wozniak hovering over an early prototype circuit board of what would become one of the first Apple computers. As Wozniak looks down at the mesh of transistors, Jobs looks directly into the camera with massive intensity. Steve Jobs is my Mentor. I have never met Steve Jobs and, at least in this life, I will never meet Steve Jobs. Nonetheless, he is my Mentor. Similarly, the fronts of your students' binders are probably plastered with the pictures of people who hold great importance to them in their lives – even if you think their choices are, at times, quite strange. They will probably never meet the people pictured behind the translucent plastic that they carry around with them each day. Yet, these Mentors whom students aspire to emulate and embody hold great importance – an importance that deserves our attention as educators developing students and each other. You don't have to meet your Mentor for that person to impact your life. These Mentors are role models, inspirers, and instructors.

My master teacher during my teacher induction was also my Mentor. She was not the best instructor with whom I had ever worked. She was not the best with students compared to other instructors of her time, though she made a life-altering impact upon me. What made her the best Mentor for me is that she took the time to understand my needs. That is, she gave me the individualized attention that I needed to succeed as a budding educator. Rather than simply "sticking to the script" of what a master teacher should say, she worked with me on the basis of my needs as an individual learner. Accordingly, I thrived because I was getting the right type of nurturing that I individually needed. This is another type of Mentor: the nurturer.

In your school family today, students, staffulty, parents, and community members of all kinds operate as Mentors, acting as role models, inspirers, instructors, and nurturers. They already are doing their work as Mentors, even without much attention or recognition from you or your school. To move to the level of the World's Greatest High School, these Mentors deserve your support. However, rather than this support being an administrative mandate that educators be unnaturally forced to pair with one another, or students being "assigned" a student-mentor whom they will only see once the entire year (though these strategies have definite merit), consider creating the conditions for Mentorship that will allow strong relationships to form. You will need to take an active role in creating these conditions and supporting them throughout the school year.

What are the conditions that you need to create? First, as discussed in the previous chapter, place successful role models at the center of everything that you do on your campus. Place the successful students, staffulty, parents, and community members in such a position that they can inspire, instruct, and nurture others at your school. If you believe that the expertise you need is already within your buildings, you will need to place these experts in a position to be leaders and supporters of others. Consider starting meetings with one of these Mentors talking about something that "clicked" or worked well for him or her. Consider bringing past successes (like graduated students) back to your school to talk about what the school family did well for them and the things that the school could improve. Consider letting the mastery of others be the centerpiece of every meeting, gathering, celebration, and game.

Second, another condition to support Mentors is to place people and financial resources on the side of Mentorship. If you have a freshman-junior/senior mentorship program on your campus, allocate more human and financial resources to support this group. If you have a student leadership program, invest there. If you have whole staff meetings that are largely a one-man or two-man show, where the information could have been easily communicated via email, change the timing and format of the meeting to allow for MANY more voices. When you invest in the forces on your campus that specifically are aiming to support fellow students, educators, parents, etc., these people get supported!

Finally, create the containers needed for Mentorship – that is, create the physical, temporal, and emotional spaces where Mentorship can thrive on your campus. Create the physical spaces that are needed to support Mentorships of all kinds. Revitalize your staff lounge by creating a place where people truly can gather together and "lounge" (e.g., buy a ping-pong table). Ask your student leadership to post WEEKLY flyers of the schedule of all club meets for that week with locations. Provide time specifically for student-mentor groups to meet with one another on a regular basis. Provide time for educators to meet in small groups. Specifically organize optional social meet-ups weeks ahead of time at a local restaurant, sporting event, or movie showing. Purchase a license to show an inspirational film to your educators, and show it to them! Creating Mentorships and enabling Mentors is not an accidental occurrence at the World's Greatest High School. Create an on-purpose, intended plan and focus for building Mentorships.

Reflection Questions

1. Who are the major Mentors at your school today? Can you name students, staff, parents, and community members?

2. If given the opportunity, who are some people on your campus who you feel would make amazing Mentors?

3. How does your school encourage and enable students to mentor other students?

4. How does your school encourage and enable staff to mentor other staff?

5. How could you reach out to those important, irreplaceable people on campus?

Deeper Considerations

In literature, film, and in the stories of old, Mentors are often found in the forms of wizards; sages; elderly priests or priestesses; alchemists; and experienced, older experts. In nearly every case, these Mentors are tied with a locale "outside the village," far from the normal bustle of activity that busies the hero each day. Jesus, for example, had a type of mentor in the form of John the Baptist – an older, New Testament prophet who spent much of his time in the wilderness. Jesus did not find John hanging out at a local coffee shop in Jerusalem – he sought him elsewhere. Gandalf (in a separate vein entirely) sought out his Mentor, Sauruman, in his tower Isengard. Simba found Rafiki, older and grayer, in his tree lair – and Timon and Pumbaa in the forest far from home, for that matter. Mentors rarely manifest themselves on the main road. Mentors dwell just off the beaten path; sometimes, they are deep in the wilderness.

As a transformation agent at your school, actively involve yourself in creating the Mentorships that will benefit you, your staffulty, your students, and your community. Quite literally, you have to get the people under your care off the blazed trail upon which they walk each day and into the separate, sacred, transformational spaces specifically fashioned to contain Mentorship. Instead of expecting Mentorship to blossom in the midst of the hallway passersby, in the minutes of restroom breaks, or in the constant throng of bored sitters in staff meetings, exercise your power to direct people away from the norm of their days into spaces you have specifically crafted for building better human beings.

Consider your greatest Mentors in your life. Where were/are they found? What brought you together? What was the physical-emotional atmosphere that held you both, that allowed for your Mentorship to develop? First, calendared events, scheduled meets, and breakaway moments are often where Mentorship begins. Create those moments where people can step out of the scheduled norm into something exciting. Sometimes, all you have to do is create a container into which people can step. Second, the physical container also holds great importance. Is the live environment set up for the type of relationship that you are hoping to build? Are all the chairs facing one person at the front of the room? How long can your butt survive in these chairs? Is this a fun place; a boring, serious place; or a sacred space where transformation is intentionally and publicly expected to happen? Finally, consider the context within which each of your students, staffulty, parents, etc. sit. Are they in pain? Are they skeptical? What are they internally experiencing together? Alone? All your Mentorship efforts must be on THEIR behalf; create a space in which each member can thrive.

Deeper Questions

1. Imagine one physical space in which large or small groups of educators could gather together on your campus to discuss life and practice. What physical characteristics would this space have? What items would it have within it? Where would it be located on your campus so that all could have access to it at will throughout the day?

2. Create a list of steps to create this space on your campus within the next fourteen days. What would have to happen to create this space? How could you make this happen?

3. What financial barriers stand in the way of making this happen? What items do you specifically need for which you need a donation? Imagine how you would reach out to various groups of supporters to assist you in getting these items.

We Dare You

If you are reading this workbook and going through these activities, you are already a budding (perhaps already established) change agent at your school. At this stage, own your role as someone who is working bravely to make your school a better place. As you have worked through these dares and as you are progressing through this workbook, each action that you take is more and more public. You are less and less the warrior alone in the classroom – you are stepping into the hallways more and more and taking direct, visible action on behalf of your school family. Already, people are noticing.

At this stage, it's worth mentioning that your bravery will not always be appreciated, respected, or welcomed. In fact, you might receive a lot of pushback. If you work at No Hope High School, many will think you are foolish. They might say, "Don't you see what kind of school this is? We have tried that already! It failed miserably before and we are just going to see it fail again!" Oh, what woe! If you work at Mediocre High School, many will think that you are trying too hard. Others will say, "We already have a good thing going here. We're okay! Why are you changing things up? Don't you see that you are making some of us uncomfortable!" Growth hurts! The path upon which you are walking will NOT be free of hardship for you, the change agent. Instead, with each step, you'll be met with a new challenge. You can run or shy away, or you can face these challenges with the bravery that is rising up within you more and more with each step. You can accept these challenges, feel their impact upon you, and allow them to be part of what fuels you forward. Walk with bravery.

This dare asks you to specifically create a targeted transformation on your campus. First, you'll be observing how things are currently playing out in a specific physical space. Then, you'll do some brainstorming about what is needed therein. Finally, you will make a change to this space that you think will have a positive impact upon your school family. Trust your instincts during this activity; your mind may try to convince you to do something logical when what is needed opposes the norm at your school. Again, bravery.

The Dare

Twice each day for the next five days, walk through the staff lounge at your school. Notice who is present and how many people are present there. Return to your normal activity for the day.

At the end of each day, answer the following questions:

1. When were people present in the staff lounge? During break times? During lunch times?

2. To the best of your knowledge, what were people doing there? Were they sitting? Standing? Gathering around a certain person or object?

3. What was the emotional feel of the room? Was it serious? Boring? Fun? Sacred?

Record your answers in your journal.

At the end of the week, answer the following questions:

1. How are emotional and physical blockages within the heart of your school preventing Mentorship from further developing in this space you observed?

2. What physical or emotional landmarks are people already gathering around in this space? The complain-fest? A circle of support? A sugary soda machine?

3. Imagine a doctor-prescribed course of action for this space and its inhabitants. What specifically do you want to inject into this space? Upon what do you wish to operate? What needs to be surgically removed?

After you have considered the answers to these questions, carry out your prescription in this space. Consider placing a coffee pot and cups in this space. Buy a ping-pong, foosball, or pool table off CraigsList.com (well worth the investment) and place it in this space. Find and insert couches, lounge chairs, throw pillows, and lamps. Advertise these new additions to this space. Repeat this dare and observe what happens. Do not shy away from changing this space.

Want to go deeper? Want to further impact your instruction, students, and school? Visit our website and sign up for more free training:

www.WorldsGreatestHighSchool.com

World's Greatest Relationships

Chapter 6

"When we work together, our value multiplies."

If Mentorships are the one-to-one associations that assist you in becoming your World's Greatest Me, relationships, in general, could be seen as the ways that your whole school family interacts with one another as a unique culture of people. Where Mentorship is between "you and I," relationships refer to the interaction of "us all." Where Mentorship refers to two, relationships, in the sense we discuss in this chapter, relate to many together. Consider: As a cadre of human beings interacting with one another each day, what kind of culture is your school embodying each day?

A singular educator, student, or parent does not craft your school's culture. Some schools into which we have stepped foot have an air of "No Hope" floating through the hallways and stagnating in the classrooms. It's not that these schools have no hope; they simply act that way together! In all the time we've spent in schools, we have never found one human being who is responsible for the suffering of an entire campus. Sure, you might know a specific person on your campus who you think should bear the brunt of the shame, but, frankly, the culture of a school is not dictated by one individual. Each day, everyone connected to your school family collectively creates your school's culture. Everyone holds a piece of the thread that weaves together to create the fabric of your school's mandala.

Your school family, however, may be acting as if "school culture" is the responsibility of one principal, assistant principal, activities director, or leadership teacher. I recall sitting in a meeting at a school I visited. The principal was leading a whole staff discussion about declining student performance. Quite openly, he asked the entire staff, "What about our school's culture is contributing to this situation?" In the minutes that followed, staff member after staff member began reiterating the same words: "Our school used to be so great! We used to be a family! We are losing our traditions! Our family here is dying." Instead, however, of that leading to staff members talking about jumping into the throng of activity, getting involved, and making the school a better place, much of the staff began pointing fingers at one another. At the World's Greatest High School, everyone has a part of building, maintaining, and advancing the culture of the school. Everyone is involved in teaching the culture of Greatness. Everyone is involved in learning it time and time again through your school's traditions, rituals, and celebrations.

A World's Greatest school culture is not created by accident; it is created, planned, taught, and reinforced continually. Over and over again, your school family must teach the culture of the school to new and old members alike. For example, staff members at one of my favorite schools in development often boast that they have the most student clubs of any high school in the area. However, when we dig deeper into the situation, we see that most clubs only meet one or two times the entire year. "We had an amazing club rush!" they say, but never were clubs advertised in the weeks after. Never again do these clubs show themselves until the beginning of the next school year. This is a failing strategy. However, one staff that is building the World's Greatest High School teaches the culture of the school from the moment that students walk into the school the first day. Seniors and juniors quite literally "induct" incoming freshmen into the school through special large-group ceremonies and small-group breakouts. Students are taught the traditions of the school and learn the symbolism of the mascot, logo, and the rest of the school brand. The culminating activity is the school's first rally, where the new freshmen compete with the rest of the classes for recognition and awards. This strategy is not an accident; school culture is taught on purpose through the power of relationships.

Park loves to tell the story of building the World's Greatest High School as activities director with his student leadership class. This group of students TAUGHT THE STAFF the school traditions when new members would join. The cultural warriors of the school were not simply the adults or the older kids; the leadership students of all ages would be active participants. Further, when the World's Greatest rallies would be held, all students (not just the leadership) would work with one another to rally the crowd to participate in the traditional, ritual, and celebratory activities that linked together the school's cultural chain. When you allow staffulty, students, and parents of all walks to teach the culture of your school, others have the benefit of a true induction into a true family. Will you allow them to teach your culture?

Consider the haves and have-nots at your school. Think about staff members, students, and parents. Who is "in" and who is "out"? How will you bring these outsiders into the family you care so much about? Families have a culture, and they teach one another that culture. How will you allow others to be part of this teaching?

Reflection Questions

1. What people and places tend to be the heart-centers of relationships and conversation at your school?

2. Who are largely or completely disconnected from relationships and conversation at your school?

3. What are some ways you could encourage "community" on your campus?

4. What are some ways that you need to simply "get out of the way"?

5. What is your relationship to your school's values, expectations, and beliefs?

6. Who teaches the culture to new members of your school? How?

7. How are the students expected to be part of the teaching of the school's culture?

8. How are you personally making strides to enhance the lives and well-being of those who teach with you?

Deeper Considerations

Traditions, celebrations, and rituals have significantly shaped me as a human being. When I was fourteen years old, just a week before starting my freshman year of high school, I took part in a one-week leadership camp with my local council of the Boy Scouts of America. The entire purpose of the camp was to induct young boys into adulthood. Quite openly, we were told that we would enter the forest as boys, but we would be emerging as young adults – "if you survive the week," the adult leaders added with a smirk. For the next seven days, I was immersed in a cultural experience – an induction into a culture of manhood that impacts me to this day.

On the first night, we were silently walked into the woods in the San Bernardino Mountains through a moonlit clearing. In the distance, we could hear the pops of a campfire, and soon we saw the glow of the flames rising in a dance of controlled chaos through the treetops. Without a word, nearly a hundred of us sat down as the cold wind began to blow through the Jeffrey Pines (which is quite a feat with ninety-something freshman boys). The eldest of the young adult leaders (about seventeen years old) emerged from the darkness and stood tall in front of the fire between us. He spent many minutes explaining the meaning of brotherhood in relationship to ourselves, our families, and our community and country. "Today," he said with proud eyes, "you begin your first steps into the brotherhood of men." To this day, I often think about the power of that moment. We were not welcomed with a handbook, schedule, or list of rules. Instead, we were invited to become better human beings – to leave boyhood behind and step into our adulthood with pride. Not a single adult leader spoke that night. Our seventeen-year-old counterparts led the entire ceremony. The relationship was established from the moment they first spoke. We were inducted into this new family. Today as a teacher, I often wonder, "How can we induct students with such effortlessness and with such prestige?"

As educators, we are witnesses to coming-of-age ceremonies of all kinds each day. We see the new freshmen entering our school. We see, with each passing grading period, students stepping further into adulthood. At graduation, our grandest ceremony, we see our students released from our container into the wide, wide world. Similarly, we see these same types of stages with our new teachers, our established educators, and our retiring or soon-to-retire friends. Our community ebbs and flows into its next stage of life with each advance or disaster. There is always movement. The question you must consider is, "How will I recognize, respond, and celebrate each movement forward?" Will you create such vital, ritual components of your school culture? How will you allow your students, staffulty, and community to take part?

Deeper Questions

1. List the essential values of your school's culture.

2. List and describe the essential traditions, celebrations, and rituals of your school's culture.

3. How do you showcase your values during/within these essential traditions, celebrations, and rituals?

4. Specifically, how could these happenings at your campus TEACH the values of your school through the power of interrelationship? Think less of "poster moments"; think more in terms of "human interactions."

We Dare You

Remember, where "Mentorship" refers to the one-to-one relationships between two people connected to your school, "relationships" (in the sense we are discussing here) refer to the way in which your school family interacts with one another together. Mentorship involves two people. The relationships to which we are referring in this chapter are the collective "we" that manifests as your school's culture. Where No Hope and Mediocre High School have "cultures by default," the World's Greatest High School's culture is crafted brick-by-brick with intentionality, creativity, and dignity. This dare will assist you in creating one meaningful manifestation of your school's culture in an exceedingly tangible way.

This dare takes place in two phases. First, you will be meeting with a representative group of your school family members and drawing out the important, essential aspects of your school's culture. Second, you will work with the same (or a similar) group of school family members to create a physical manifestation of your culture that impacts EVERY single person connected to your school. Long story short: when you complete the last steps of this dare, you'll want to bring a camera – it's going to be amazing.

Prework & Preparation

Before we begin, here are some notes. First and foremost, it will be tempting to skip this preparation for the big part of the dare that appears on the next page. Know that if you skip this section, you are not going to experience the transformation that you seek for your school to the degree that you wish. DO THIS! Second, there are some essential players that MUST be part of this process; they are (1) a student leadership teacher or activities director, (2) and student leaders. If you cannot get access to (or you are not one of) these people, you'll need to pause here and form your own rag-tag group of World's Greatest High School builders.

With a representative group of your school family members (preferably about twenty people), including students, staffulty, parents, and community partners, meet in a room together. Bring food and drinks. Have people sit in mixed groups (student, parent, staff, community member) of four throughout the room. Place poster paper at the center of every group with a pile of markers. Ask them the "Deeper Questions" from the previous page, having them DRAW their answers as a group on the poster paper. Play music while they are drawing. Allow three to five minutes per question. Repeat for all the questions listed. Then, circle all chairs in the room as a whole group. Showcase and discuss the answers. Note all the common sentiments.

The Dare

Each day for the next seven days, work with a group of student leaders to DESIGN a whole-school gathering (rally, promotion, celebration) based upon the information that you gathered during the Prework and Preparation.

Hang the posters that your team created during the Prework and Preparation throughout your workspace as inspiration.

Before you begin designing, answer these essential questions as a whole group of leaders. Record your answers on a board or poster papers:

1. During this gathering, what three to six essential values of our school will we showcase?

2. During this gathering, how will we celebrate people who have lived out these values in their daily lives?

3. During this gathering, how will we specifically celebrate students, staffulty, parents, AND community partners?

4. After this gathering, what is ONE BIG MESSAGE that we hope people take away with them?

5. What is the one-word emotional description of this gathering?

The answers to these questions are the major anchor points for the gathering you are designing. Make sure you consider these for EVERY aspect of the gathering.

Next, as you are creating the blueprint for this gathering, consider these often ignored aspects. Consider: How will each of the following elements connect to the answers you gave above?

Music	Meaningful student-led activities
Grand entrance	Ritual
Grand exit	Coming of age
Transcendent moments	Passing the torch
Smells	Showcasing gifts, talents, skills
Seating arrangement	SHOW our values
VIP seating	Our champions
Stories	Our story of struggle
Microphone moments	World's Greatest Me

Want to go deeper? Want to further impact your instruction, students, and school? Visit our website and sign up for more free training:

www.WorldsGreatestHighSchool.com

World's Greatest Planning

Chapter 7

"When you plan for the success of a few, few will be successful."

How are our plans as educators predetermining outcomes for our students? One local high school has an honor roll and academic recognition program. Of the two thousand students, one hundred qualify to be recognized. Another campus just down the street has the same achievement programs and nearly the same number of students attending, but this school has over five hundred students qualifying and being recognized. When we hear about these two schools – one having 400% more students being recognized for their academic achievement – we could easily say, "Wow, clearly the students at School X are doing so much better than the students at School Y!" On the surface, we see the difference in numbers and shake our heads. However, if we visited the campus with the greater number of "successful" students, we'd see something worth considering: while a student's personal behavior and determination have much to do with his or her success, it's the school that often determines the degree to which the student will be celebrated, recognized, and affirmed for that behavior. Student success is already there, if we have the eyes to see it.

Even in the most challenged schools, there are successful students. One school that I visited had security officers in the parking lot to ensure staff property could sit without incident. The outside of the school looked more fortified than most police departments. Inside, students walked in large groups around campus long after the bell had rung. However, when I stepped inside their newly-established, budding student leadership classroom, my heart began to open, my ears began to listen, and I met some of the amazing students who wanted to make this place the best school for their community's teenagers. One student I met has long stuck in my mind, bending my old definition of success. On nearly all counts, this student was not the traditional "success" of any school. His GPA was quite low. His test scores were horrible. He was not on track to graduate on time. However, this guy, for the first time probably ever in his high school career, had shown up to school on time, without an absence, for the last thirty days of school. This leadership class spent the entire first five minutes of class going to this student's first period and giving him breakfast and applause for showing up. The school would normally have ignored this student. These student leaders, however, were not going to let that happen. They showed this student that they saw how he was becoming his World's Greatest Me every day. You can choose to recognize only your top twenty-five students – or you can decide to expand your vision and see more of the successes that are happening at your school and recognize those too. You can expand how you see (or recognize) these many successes at your school.

Educators have missed what recognition truly means. Think about the word, "recognition." Pause and think about that... What images come to your mind? Most educators think of recognition as a piece of paper, or a medal, or a name on a wall. They think of gifts. Also, they think of ceremonies with dozens of students getting these gifts. They see long lists of names on scrolls or programs. This is a skewed vision of true recognition. This is like saying that "love" is giving roses or throwing your sweetie a birthday party – as if true love were something done *to* or *for* someone. True recognition means "true seeing." When you are recognizing student success in this way, you are creating transcendent moments where the student experiences others seeing his or her World's Greatest Me. In this way, you are crafting moments where the student can experience the "reinforcement" of others truly seeing this student for what he or she is – a young person who is trying to better his or her life. The ultimate reward is not a piece of paper that goes home and ends up buried under a pile of homework or put into a drawer. The ultimate reward that you can give students is a moment where they experience being truly seen for who they are and what they are doing. Educators can truly recognize their students by creating these transcendent moments of being seen.

Consider how your school plans for the successes of students. What avenues of success are already available for students? Does your school recognize improvement? When and how does it do that? If you wrote down all the different types of successes that your school already celebrates, what types of successes would be missing? With so much emphasis being placed on "planning" by schools and school districts throughout the country, our greatest hope is that educators recognize the self-fulfilling prophecy that is created by the paths of success they create on their campuses. When you plan for the success of a few, a few will be successful. However, when you expand your vision for seeing success on your campus and show others that you are seeing them be successful by this expanded definition, you are more able to induct these people into the main paths that you've established for them at your school. Why make graduation the first time a student is truly seen as an individual at your school? Create transcendent moments throughout his or her high school career, where the student can be seen regularly for being his or her World's Greatest Me.

Reflection Questions

1. As an educator, how do you know when an individual student has advanced his or her unique skills? To what evidence do you typically look? What evidence do you typically ignore?

2. In what ways does your school treat students as "groups of kids," as opposed to "individual students"?

3. What are some examples of student success on campus that you don't often see being broadcasted or celebrated?

4. If you were to make an educated guess, what would be your school's unique definition of success?

Deeper Considerations

Transcendent moments are worth creating in our world and capturing in our hearts. What mammoth changes have you endured in the past five years of your life? The past ten years? When you are thirty, forty, or fifty years old, the years move differently than when you were younger. When you were fifteen, five years was a third of your life! When you were ten, five years was HALF your life! Our way of seeing and relating to our development as people is often most clear in hindsight. It's with the passage of time, and the wisdom that hopefully brings us, that we can see things as they were – or at least how we believe they were. When we sit with educators and ask them about the experiences that made them into the human beings they are today, it's not uncommon to hear them say, "I wish I knew then what I know now. I wish that I knew how special and precious those moments were as I lived them." What would it have been like to know the importance of the high school journey that you were walking when you were walking it? What would that have allowed you to have, be, and do that was otherwise unavailable to you? Consider: Your students could benefit today by experiencing grand episodes of their daily quest to become the World's Greatest Me. You simply have to create these moments and encourage them to see the importance.

Moments of importance must first be created. As an educator, you know that the seasons of your school move through your classrooms, activities, and instruction without much fanfare. You feel the rush of September, the intensity of October, the desire in November for December, the easing into the break during December – all preparing you for the push through April and May. You don't experience this alone; your students are going along right there with you on this track toward the year to come. Unless you craft these transcendent moments for students to experience, creating something worth noticing, your school family will simply keep going about business as usual. Mass printings of certificates are boring. Medals given out in mass without a heart connection are expensive and nearly meaningless. Achievement cards that have no benefit to students have no significance to students. Create something worth noticing. Create something that points to something meaningful: a student changing his or her life for the better. Show a student that you see him or her becoming a better human being. Planning of this kind requires that you focus less on groups of students and more on individuals. Further, to create transcendent moments of this kind, you must have students notice regular story points along the journey. Your students will love graduation (the finale) in an entirely different way when they have been reminded along the way of how far they have come. Will you provide such reminders to show students the grand journey they are walking?

Deeper Questions

1. Thinking of the youngest students on your campus, what are the major plot points of their journey through their first year? Consider: What big life lessons must they endure during each of these seasons?

	Plot Points	Lessons
Beginning of the year –		
Middle of the year –		
End of the year –		

2. Thinking of the students in the middle age group on your campus, what are the major plot points of their journey through their middle years? Consider: What big life lessons must they endure during each of these seasons?

	Plot Points	Lessons
Beginning of the year –		
Middle of the year –		
End of the year –		

3. Thinking of the eldest students on your campus, what are the major plot points of their journey through their final year? Consider: What big life lessons must they endure during each of these seasons?

	Plot Points	Lessons
Beginning of the year –		
Middle of the year –		
End of the year –		

www.worldsgreatesthighschool.com   61

We Dare You

In this chapter of this workbook, we have pointed to a few important concepts. First, we discussed how student success is already present at your school – more than you probably are currently seeing. Usually, educators only see a relatively small number of the daily miracles happening on campus each day. We presented the notion that if you have the eyes to see these successes, they will not only appear to you, but you will be more able to support these students in furthering their success. Second, we pointed to how school families often treat "recognition" as a thing done *to* someone ("We recognized them!" handing them a piece of mass-printed certificate paper). We talked about how true recognition is, really, true seeing: seeing students for who they are and what they are doing AND having them experience you and others seeing them for who they truly are. This instance, where a student sees others truly seeing him or her being his or her World's Greatest Me, is a transcendent moment. Finally, we presented the idea that you can create transcendent moments for your students. Moments such as these can be manufactured simply from the raw materials that already make up students' tenure at your school. Already, they are enduring major plot points in their journey toward graduation. Already, they are learning the lessons such travelers learn upon this kind of journey. All you have to do is create these "look at me" moments and enable students to have their hearts captured in the process – not easy, but exceedingly rewarding.

This dare is ALL about you creating transcendent moments for your students. First, you will construct transcendent moments for a small handful of students in your classroom or on your caseload. Second, you will expand your creative ability to a larger group of students, hopefully with the assistance of fellow staff members or student leaders. Finally, you will ultimately expand your capacity to create transcendent moments to the level of the whole school. Unlike previous dares, which were accomplished within five to seven days, this will take a much greater time commitment. We encourage you to not walk this road alone as you are working on this aspect of building your World's Greatest High School. Team up with like-minded individuals who can assist you. Further, please do not solely rely upon the student leaders who are so willing to ally with you. Rely also upon the partnerships you can build with other educators in your midst. Get out of your cave! As you embark upon this dare, imagine: What would it be like to walk into a place each morning that *could* profoundly, authentically claim on its gates, "Welcome to the World's Greatest High School"? If you have this vision for your school, create a place where the people and heart-capturing moments within justify such a proclamation.

The Dare

Phase One

Examine your answers to the "Deeper Questions" in this chapter. Each day for the next five days, notice times when a specific student is enduring, experiencing, or embodying the "plot points" experienced by many other students of that age.

Twice each day, when you notice these instances, approach the specific student and say something to the effect of, "Jan, I notice that you are [insert plot point here]. Clearly you are [describe specific behavior he or she is doing or the quality he or she is embodying]. I just want to say that I recognize how hard you are working and that it is not unnoticed." Let this be a short, poignant moment. Then, go about your normal daily activity.

Phase Two

After completing the above phase, doing the above action for five days, complete this second phase of the dare. Teach the first-phase activity to a group of fellow staff members or student leaders. Over the next five days, have them perform the dare. At the end of the week, meet together and answer the following questions:

1. To what degree were students caught up in the transcendent moment that you were creating with/for them? What physical and emotional reactions did you notice?

2. To what degree were you recognizing (or seeing) something that would have otherwise gone unseen?

3. As a whole school, how could we more publicly and more regularly "see" our students?

As a whole group, carefully consider: How could you allow more people to be "seen" publicly, regularly in meaningful ways? Brainstorm on this issue.

Phase Three

After completing the previous phases of this dare, gather together a core group of fellow educators and student leaders. Utilizing the same method of planning from the dare in Chapter 6 (the previous chapter), how could you create transcendent moments, where students are authentically seen for being their World's Greatest Me, into a public celebration? Design a new celebration/ritual or modify an existing celebration/ritual to embed public moments of "being seen" for your students.

Want to go deeper? Want to further impact your instruction, students, and school? Visit our website and sign up for more free training:

www.WorldsGreatestHighSchool.com

World's Greatest Branding

Chapter 8

"Is your one-of-a-kind school expressing itself in a one-of-a-kind way?"

Are you simply changing the wallpaper, or are you building a stronger foundation for your school? In *Building the World's Greatest High School*, we defined branding the feelings, names, symbols, and slogans used to identify a product. Since the book was published, we have had the opportunity to see the ways in which educators have interacted with this definition, the "Blueprint Questions," and the dares found within the master text. Often, we see unfolding stories where educators have started to ask what kind of product the school is creating (what kind of student emerges from their school). These educators are making concerted efforts to make success the norm for those who walk through their halls. They focus on what is authentically happening, and they seek to change *that*. Some educators are simply changing the looks of things – they are changing the wallpaper. Little is truly changing. Behind the posters, behind the balloons, and behind the doors of the governing student body, things are "business as usual." Branding is not about looks; instead, branding reflects authentic expressions of who you are and what you are truly doing as a whole school.

I recently visited a school that is wrestling with the difference between (1) inauthentically changing the wallpaper to make things look better, and (2) authentically building a strong foundation for the school that will naturally show the amazing things happening within. Each individual faction within has sought to better the image of the school in its own way. Three factions have created separate logos for the school that are displayed on shirts, helmets, and banners. A number of departments have adopted strong policies about student work that each displays on the school's website. Hundreds of thousands of dollars have been spent on upgraded facilities. The walls are freshly painted, the shirts and banners are hot off the presses, and the parking lot is adorned with new gates and proud signage; within, however, nothing much has changed. The teaching is relatively the same. The staffulty for the most part does not believe in the possibility of success for all students. These educators' outer game looks cleaner than before (it's fresh paint, after all); but their inner game has barely changed. Despite all the hundreds, thousands, or even millions of dollars that your school could spend on "improving facilities," unless you improve the hearts of those who are teaching and leading at your school (and thereby work to change the hearts of your learners), you are only changing the artwork on the wall.

Heart shifts often are heralded by dramatic outer shifts. In mythology, people who made contact with the divine exhibited signs of their transformation. Their faces shined. Their names were changed. They brought with them talismans and artifacts from beyond the natural world. Often, they bore the battle scars (inside and out) of their travels. I liken it to meeting career soldiers out of uniform: often you can tell that they carry with them the lessons learned on the battlefield, even though they are not wearing a dress uniform adorned with medals. Their wisdom is in their bodies; not displayed with bragging pride. True masters do not seek to change their appearance; instead, they seek true awakening within their discipline, and their bodies are changed naturally. Are your fellow educators working to change the appearance of things? Alternatively, are they seeking a true awakening as teachers? Begin by changing your way of teaching within your classroom. Then, assist others in changing their way of teaching in theirs. Students will naturally be bettered. The school will naturally show it is better. Then, put up a banner to celebrate.

A dear friend who teaches in Southern California was able to create this shift in a matter of weeks. She presented the World's Greatest Values to her administration and staff, beginning a true conversation about what "all students have futures" means. She began having this same conversation with her student leaders, asking them what it means to be student leaders in a school that holds such strong values about teaching and learning. Parents and community members began to be involved. These conversations continued, the fruits of which began to manifest inside and outside the classroom. Within a few weeks after my friend brought the idea of the World's Greatest High School to her junior high school, at her opening dance celebration for her students, one student, who had started at the school only days before, stood up at the microphone and proclaimed "I was so nervous coming to this campus, but I truly can say that this is the World's Greatest Junior High. Thank you for welcoming me." This moment of authentic expression was not the byproduct of a poster, a logo, or a freshly painted gym; this was the natural outpouring of emotion from a student who was experiencing something real happening at this school.

Rather than spending so much time and energy on changing the artwork on your walls, spend time truly mastering the teaching and learning at your school. When you begin to further master these critical components of creating amazing graduates and World's Greatest Educators, the world around you will see authentic expressions of who you are everywhere. Then, as this transformation occurs, begin spreading the message of this shift on your walls, letterhead, apparel, and beyond.

Reflection Questions

1. Thinking about the definition we presented at the start of this chapter, what branding already exists at your school? Make a list.

2. To what "interest" or "faction" does each feeling, name, symbol, and slogan belong?

3. Do these belong to the whole school or just one group?

4. Who are key persons attached to each of these?

5. What does each piece of branding communicate to the community about your school?

6. What does each piece of branding indicate you value as a school?

Deeper Considerations

All cultures have their champions, but, often, school families have amnesia. Schools are filled with heroes of the week who are quickly forgotten – only the "great ones" are remembered forever. The memory of most schools is only the span of about four years or so. Consider the name of the valedictorian from three years ago. This person was the best student around, and you probably cannot remember his or her name right now. Consider the teacher who won Most Inspirational Teacher of the Year two years ago; do you remember that name? What about the person or place for which your school is named? How did that come about? What did you have for lunch yesterday? Cultures have a history; they have a story of transformation and heroes who were the champions of this great shift. Without such heroes being recognized and remembered, there is not much of a story. People forget. People stagnate. People feel depressed. "Today is just another day at Mediocre High." If you are a champion for your school's culture, then you have the power to create heroes and ensure that they are remembered.

Stories of heroism are around you each day. When we survey students about successes on their campus, we often meet students who are keenly aware of someone around them has gone through great struggle into greatness. We hear about students who sleep in a field each night yet show up on time, without fail, to class each morning. We hear about students who lost a sibling yet have increased their GPA 100% in the past two semesters. We hear about students whose parents never finished middle school, yet those students just applied to some of the best schools in the state. These kinds of stories are in the ether; they are everywhere, just waiting for you to tap into them, sharpen them, and retell them in a compelling way within your school culture.

You must have heroic eyes. As we have discussed in many of our writings and stated in our live trainings, we have the ability, as educators, to work with our students as individual human beings, seeing the unique contribution that each person is making to our campus each day. It takes courage to see students in this way. It requires that we become closer to and more vulnerable around our students. It requires that we become the best listeners possible. It requires us to step into the role of mentorship that "teaching" is truly calling us to embody. When you begin to listen with more courageous ears and see with more heroic eyes, you can see successes everywhere on your campus. Then, when you see such a success, learn the story behind the brave actions of students. As you are listening to them, remember the bravery that they must have simply to show up each day.

Deeper Questions

1. Considering a student, educator, or parent, describe a single, tangible story of success on your campus.

2. In what ways is this story, authentically, a great example of the values of your school in action?

3. How could you make this type of success the norm on your campus?

We Dare You

"History," in the sense that we are discussing, does not emerge naturally within schools. Instead, the history of the heroes of your school has to be cultivated, recorded, and broadcasted over and over again. There are many ways that you can go about doing this. Park has said for some time that celebrations are one way that you can ritualize the history of your school, the values you hold, and the emerging stories of success within (and without). I say that rites of passage should always be moderated and facilitated by those who have "gone before." The elders of your community should lead (if not organize, structure, and carry out) rites of passage, regardless of whether they are eighteen years old or seventy years old. Regardless of how you codify (gather together) your history and get it in front of the eyes of your students, parents, staffulty, and community partners, the necessary ingredients are "intention" and "elders."

First, let's say a few brief words about intention. Intention could be simply defined as "doing something on purpose." That's exactly what we are asking you to do in this dare: to create a recapitulation of the history of your school *on purpose*. Nothing in the presentation will be by accident, save the potential extraordinary moment that could emerge naturally within the retelling of your school's history. A ritual that reinforces history has the strong backbone of tradition holding it together. Many of you will be creating something from scratch, so you'll have to be in all the details of putting together the type of grand moment that we will be describing in this dare. Leave little to chance in this dare. The stronger you prepare for and execute this dare, the bigger the impact on those who witness it. We dare you to intentionally put this thing together as if it were the second most important event to your graduation.

Second, a word about elders: don't put your aging elders alone on a boat and send them into the ocean and fog, never to return. Instead, build a warm place where they can interact with those in your school family, and give them a forum to speak. These elders could be recent graduates; they could be graduates of many years past. They could be teachers. It could be the person for whom the school was named. It could be a person of any kind who is connected to your school in some way. Give them a microphone moment. Have their words be what reinforces what you and your school are trying to accomplish. This dare will ask you to do something that many of us do not do in our lives: honor the elders of our community, give them a voice, and put them in a place of honor at the center of conversation. They hold your history in their hearts. Let them speak it.

The Dare

Over the next week, take at least fifteen minutes each day to interview one or more educators, asking them the following questions:

1. Thinking back, who are the past heroes of our school? What made each a hero? Do you know how we could contact them?

2. What heroes have we forgotten altogether? What made each a hero? Do you know how we could contact them?

3. How should we publicly honor these heroes?

Ask these questions of staffulty of all levels of seniority. Remember, each person will have a different expertise about a specific time period of your school's history.

Next, each day over the following week, make contact with at least one of these heroes mentioned above. Ask them the following questions:

1. When we spoke to X, they said that you were a hero of the school because of Y. What do you think about that? What could you tell us about that time of our school?

2. Thinking back, who are the past heroes of our school? What made each a hero? Do you know how we could contact them?

3. What heroes have we forgotten altogether? What made each a hero? Do you know how we could contact them?

4. How should we publicly honor these heroes?

Finally, utilizing your skills of creating an event or ritual reinforced earlier in this workbook, build and execute a gathering of your staffulty, students, and/or community partners that will accomplish the following goals:

1. Honor these heroes;

2. Provide these heroes with a microphone moment to speak about what's great about your school and its history;

3. Reinforce the values of your school, how these heroes lived them out, and how new heroes are living out these values today *already* at your school.

This event is an optimal time to induct these heroes into your hall of fame (whether it exists or not) and to permanently memorialize these people with a plaque or photo alongside their story. You'll invite them back to speak again!

Want to go deeper? Want to further impact your instruction, students, and school? Visit our website and sign up for more free training:

www.WorldsGreatestHighSchool.com

World's Greatest Marketing

Chapter 9

"Market the futures of your students."

In the previous chapter, we posed the idea that branding is simply authentic expressions of who you are and what you are truly doing as a whole school. In a perfect world, these authentic expressions would systematically find their way to every important eyeball, ear, and heart inside and outside your campus. In this magical, make-believe world, people would automatically see the World's Greatest happening at your school and want to join in. Naturally, this is not what happens. Instead, the message needs to be purposefully cross-pollinated between the social networks connected to your campus. When we say social networks, we are not talking just about those online things that your school district has banned. By social networks, we mean the masses of connected human beings who are already walking through your halls, working in businesses outside your school, and driving right now on the freeway to God-knows-where. All these people are connected to your school. Marketing, then, is the intentional injecting of your school's brand into the various living systems connected to your school. Let's look at some of these living systems.

First, there are the individual hearts that are walking around your campus right now. Each person has an inner world that needs to be cultivated by you and your school family so that the person can become his or her World's Greatest Me. Every moment of every day, each of these students, parents, staffulty, and community partners are making inner-game decisions that directly impact their work (or lack thereof) on or connected to your campus. How will you ensure that the great work that your school is doing reaches the inner world of these people?

Second, another living system at your school is found in the daily routines, schedules, policies, and procedures enacted by your school as a community. The bell schedule is an expression of this living system. If you don't believe us, simply stand in the middle of the quad as the lunch bell rings; you'll see a whole array of living activity spring to life, simply because your school has decided to play a sound at a particular time of the morning. The way that your school handles discipline as a whole is an expression of this type of living system. How will you ensure that the World's Greatest Values that your school is attempting to live out are alive within this system?

How will your school's authentic expression of itself be found within the policies and procedures that make your school collectively function?

Finally, there is the cultural living system at work in your school. This culture is created through all the hearts of all the individuals walking through your halls feeling in unison. You can see this most by asking a few dozen people, "What kind of school are we?" If enough people say, "We are the runt of the school district," you can believe that this is a component of the culture of your school. If enough people say, "We are the kind of school that is filled with people becoming their best selves," you can believe that your school is on its way to becoming the World's Greatest High School. How will you ensure that the great work of your school is part of the felt experience of all persons on your campus?

When most people think about marketing, they think about ways to "get the word out" about something that happened or will happen in the future. This approach is solely focused on eyes and ears – hoping that people will do something in the future. This is an exceedingly shallow approach, especially when we are talking about school change. If your student leaders are spending most of their time getting the word out about activities on campus, they are missing out on something paramount to your school's potential growth: inducting others into your school family.

Do you have a family tradition? Growing up, my family's tradition was going on a road trip each summer. My father would pack us into our fifth-wheel trailer and drive all over the United States. Did my father hang up a poster outside my bedroom each June in preparation for our departure? Did I receive a photocopied flyer each Monday morning to remind me about our impending departure? Of course not. Our family did road trips; it was a natural part of being in the family. However, one summer, when one of our extended family members was going to join us on the road for the first time, there was a whole process that was set in motion to get him prepared to be part of our family's tradition. He had to be trained. He had to be oriented to our way of travel. He needed the basic information. He had to experience our first night on the road to truly see what this whole tradition was all about. He had to be inducted into our family in a way he had never been before.

Think about marketing as inducting people into the school family. That is, marketing is about allowing people to experience what it is like to be part of the school family in a way they have never been before. You are teaching these new family members everything it means to be part of your school. You have to teach them! When people arrive to your family's "home" (school) for the first time, how do you greet them? How do you induct them in? How do you make them family?

Reflection Questions

1. Thinking of the last school celebration you attended, what successes were celebrated there?

2. What are the ways in which your school already teaches your school's brand to your students?

3. What is one school celebration that could be enhanced to provide more epic podium moments to showcase stories of struggle and triumph?

Deeper Considerations

Today, your school's culture is probably in one of three categories. First, perhaps your school feels the weight of all the challenges that it is facing. People say, "You don't understand our kids. Many will never succeed." This school culture is living out the way of No Hope High School. As things stand, little will change. Things may just get worse. We have walked onto many of these campuses; it's a sad sight. Second, perhaps your school feels that it is okay being okay. People say, "We are just fine where we are. I think we are doing okay. We have some successes and we have some failures. There's nothing really to fuss about. We'll be just fine." This school culture could be called Mediocre High. People here will not move ahead because they are comfortable and/or resigned to how the school is doing. Finally, there are those school family members who are working together each day to become their World's Greatest Me. These people band together to live out their best selves. We call this school the World's Greatest High School. What an amazing place! Regardless of which category your school fits into, notice how each of these types of school can be quickly distilled into feelings associated with each (No Hope, Mediocre, World's Greatest). School cultures are complex yet always have essential components. Can you distill your school's culture and identify the elements that make it up? There are three elements of a school culture that are worth examining here.

First, consider the essential traditions of your school. What do they say about student success? For example, if your most honored tradition at your school is the graduation ceremony, what messages does that ceremony send about how each student's success is valued? In *Building the World's Greatest High School* we mentioned one school that organizes the graduation by the GPA of each student. Imagine being the last guy up to the stage. What kind of message does that send? Another school has the mentor teacher of each student hand them their diploma. What message does that send? Traditions say MUCH about the essential elements of your school culture. Traditions speak to what your school values as a whole.

Second, think about the stories of success that are repeated over and over again on your school campus. Are there recent stories? Are the only success stories twenty or more years old? What does that communicate about your school's culture? What recent successes are discussed? Who enjoyed these successes? To whom do these successes and heroes belong?

Finally, reflect upon the character traits of successful students at your campus. You may even have a school mission or value statement that discusses these. Do students live these out each day? Are these truly part of your culture?

Deeper Questions

1. What are the essential three to five traditions of your school that relate to all school family members?

2. What are the essential three to five stories of success about your school that should be known by all school family members? What lesson does each teach?

3. What are the essential three to five character traits embodied within successful students at your school? (For example, perseverance, nobility, etc.)

4. Currently, how does your school induct new members into the family? What roles do the above traditions, stories, and character traits play within that induction?

We Dare You

As you were completing the questions on the previous page, you may have thought to yourself, "Wow, this is really hard! For all these being 'essential' things, they sure seem hard to boil down and write in a small space like this." If you had that experience, you are like most schools with which we work: For all the massive myriad of activity in which our schools engage each day, it is very hard to distill everything down to simple statements about who we are and what we do. Things feel much more complicated than that! Frankly, the reason that it is so hard to talk about one's school is that things may be TOO complicated – so complicated and disorganized that it is exceedingly hard to make small gains.

With all that is battling for the attention of your administrators, teachers, parents, paraeducators, students, and community partners, the school is doing so much that the essential purpose for your school may be entirely ungraspable. If you walk into most school offices in the United States, there are often framed mission statements that attempt to codify the purpose of the school into a single sentence. Sadly, we often see a lengthy sentence that is called a "mission statement" that often means nothing to most people at the school. If that mission were so important, would most of the staff not be able to recite it? Truly, if you want your students to be successful, should they not be able to tell you in a simple and succinct way WHAT their success will look like? How can your teachers be successful when they cannot define in absolutely clear terms what 'success' looks like for them? Finally, if you want to perfect your school, should you not first capture its essence so that you can augment it?

This chapter's dare asks you to draw together all that you are trying to do and be at your school, codifying it into a single sheet of paper. It is going to be tempting to write this "one-sheet" in such a way that it only belongs to a select few teachers and students. That is, you could easily write this in a way that only would appeal to the top twenty-five students at your school or the top educators who are always up for leading the next innovation at your site. Work with a group of people who represent a cross section of all the interests within your school. This will not be easy by any means. It takes intense courage to do "less" better. It takes fearlessness to be specific about what your school wants to be and how it wants to do its daily work. This is your opportunity to draw together many of the gains that you have made in previous dares and distill these into a single sheet of paper. Consider how a unified message about your school could improve your ability to induct new family members in a meaningful way.

The Dare

Create a one-sheet message about your school utilizing the following format. Meet with a group of students, educators, parents, and community partners who represent many interests within your school. Do not do this activity alone! (Extra credit: sign up for our email newsletter using the information on the following page and reply to our email with a copy of your one sheet.) Here are the elements of this one sheet:

School Name

In one sentence, describe who your school is and what it does. Keep this in the simplest terms possible.

(For example: "We help our family members become the best versions of themselves each day.")

Our Story

In 250 words or less, describe the top three to five achievements of your school in the last ten years. Consider describing the beginning, middle, and future of your school's story. Show the struggle and the story connected to the triumphs.

Our Values

In the most basic terms possible, what are the five (or so) values that your school family attempts to live out each day?

Our Traditions

In the most basic terms possible, what three to five traditions will every school family member will take part in during their tenure here? Describe each in a single sentence. Emphasize how this tradition is a vital part of your school's learning experience.

Some of Our Heroes

In the most basic terms possible, name three to five notable heroes of your school from the past five years. For each, describe their heroic story in three sentences.

How We Induct New Family Members

In five or so simple sentences, describe what steps student and teacher leaders will take to induct each new family member into your school each school year. Consider making separate lists for student leaders and teacher leaders.

Want to go deeper? Want to further impact your instruction, students, and school? Visit our website and sign up for more free training:

www.WorldsGreatestHighSchool.com

World's Greatest You

Chapter 10

"The first step in building the World's Greatest High School is building a better you from the foundation up."

By holding this page and reading this passage, you are part of a revolution. You care about your students, your fellow educators, your students' parents, and your community – in other words, your whole school family – in a way quite different from many people around you. It's revolutionary for an educator to take the time to read about and participate in activities such as these for the betterment of his or her whole school. Our hope is that through the readings and activities in this workbook, you have found a more full vision of what is happening right in front of you already and a more profound dream for your legacy of membership within your school family. We hope you have a better eye for the "now" and the "yet to come."

"Now" is an amazing yet scary place to be. When our hearts begin to open and we begin to experience *this* moment as it truly is, this can be both an exciting and a very scary place. I recall the day that I dropped all the acting like I was a "good teacher" and decided to spend the whole day actually admitting to myself when I did not have it all together. That day was the first of many days of instruction where my students felt more receptive and open to me than ever before. Because they saw my curiosity and my vulnerability, while seeing me still being strong, I felt more respect and witnessed more learning than I previously thought possible. Now is where the action is, because your students don't need you yesterday or tomorrow, they need you right here and right now. Many of the activities within this workbook were specifically crafted to get you present and catch you in that uncomfortable zone where growth occurs. Becoming a great teacher does not happen in a cabin retreat, alone with a warm fire. Instead, it happens in our classrooms, right in that moment where something is not clicking, and yet we decide to face the discomfort, feel it, and let it be our guide. Your students need you right now. You need you right now (as silly as that may seem). Will you meet yourself with kindness and openhearted curiosity, even when things are heavy and uncomfortable? We hope that, slowly, you'll be able to lower your armor and be brave not only with yourself privately but also with your students and the rest of your school family. The whole educator leadership experience changes when we can be okay with and meet this kind of discomfort.

Yet still, while we hope that you are more keen-eyed to what is happening right now in your school, we also hope that you have a grander dream about what could be for you and your school family. When I was twenty-four years old and had just become a teacher, my vision of what was possible was only as big as what I had seen before. Since then, my imagination has expanded not only to the point of all the amazing work that I have seen other school families do, but it has expanded beyond, to a realm of dreaming of which you are getting a taste here in this workbook. Throughout the reading and the activities in which you have found yourself immersed over these past many pages, we know that you have had many ideas emerge. That's one of the amazing results of dreaming: we start to rethink (or envision for the first time) our legacy for our school family. We begin to ask ourselves, "What could I give to my school family that would last far beyond my tenure here? What is going to be my contribution to this place?" These questions are not just about what is possible right now; they are pointing to something that has to be built over time with MANY hands and hearts being involved.

When I consider the legacy that I am building with others within my school family, I envision a distant shore to which we are all traveling together. Not all of us will reach that shore together, but we will fight as much as we possibly can to assist one another along the way. This journey is not one that is done over a weekend, at a weeklong professional development training, or in a singular staff meeting one dreary Friday morning. Instead, to reach this shore, we will have to work for years, through many dark times, through a handful of triumphs and a thousand failures. We do all this because of the grand dream that lies just over the water. That place is a magical one, where the mundane is transformed into gold. Pause for a moment and think about this place: What is your nearly impossible dream for your school family? Will you dare to take the years-long journey to get there? The choice is yours.

One morning, early in my teaching career, I realized that I was only responsible for being the best version of myself for me, my students, and the rest of my school family *today*. I did not have to be perfect. I did not have to be my best all the time. I simply was being called to be my best now – *right now*. Though that dream of that distant shore (that huge contribution you wish to make to your school) is a long ways away, you have the power to get a few steps closer right now. All you have to do is know which direction to walk and take a purposeful step in that direction. You don't have to know it all. You don't have to be everything to everyone. Simply be one step better than the day before. Be today's best for your students right now.

Reflection Questions

1. What do you want to have in your life as a whole?

2. What do you want to do in your life?

3. Who and/or what do you want to be?

4. What legacy would you like to leave when you retire from teaching?

Deeper Considerations

What are the conditions that must exist in your life for something new to come into it? When I was a young teacher, I recall the feeling of being in my classroom, still finishing my teaching credential, facing all the requirements that the state and my school were placing upon me. There was very little room for anything else. Even my teaching was limited by all the paperwork I was completing and all the requirements that I had to fulfill. Physically, I was exhausted. Emotionally, I was closed down. My cup was full and it could hold nothing more.

Consider all that you are holding right now that is taking up your time, energy, emotions, and physical space. What are all the things that you are holding right now that make up the daily busyness of being you? Your workplace has you holding many things on your plate. You have students. You have parents. You have fellow educators. You have paperwork. You have events to plan, meetings to make, and professional development outings to take. Your home life probably also adds many dimensions to your life. You may have pets or other humans to care for. You may have rent or a mortgage. You have this physical set of rooms that you (at least ideally) must clean from time to time. You probably have friends, peers, a lover (or lovers), and significant others who also add more and more to your personal plate. With so much vying for your attention and energy, what are you giving up? What slips through your fingers simply because you do not have the space or capacity to hold anything else right now?

There is great power in the words "No more!" not simply because they allow us to take less and less onto our shoulders. In fact, when we start narrowing down what we are doing to the most poignant elements, we start seeing gems emerge. "No more!" allows for the possibility that we can let the dirt fall away so the diamonds can show. Park and I have both been approached many times within our careers as educators by well-meaning administrators who were looking for one of us to serve on a committee or head up a program on campus. Many times, these were golden opportunities that we seized, because we knew that they aligned with our grand vision, our nearly impossible dream for our school. Many times, we said no to those requests that simply did not fit. Think about how the best placed "yes" or "no" could allow the gems of life to emerge in your day. For me, my calling is to teach, so I know that nearly anything that takes me away from the classroom is an easy "no." You may see glimmers of what you are being called to take up in your life and be faced with the reality that you must first let go of some of the extraneous weight that you are holding in your hands. Is it time to let something go?

Deeper Questions

1. What do you have or do in your life that is not sourcing (nourishing) you?

2. In what ways are these things draining energy from your life? Where could this energy be going to serve you better?

3. Speculate: How would your daily activities within your school family be more fulfilling and meaningful if some of these draining forces were eliminated from your life?

We Dare You

The purpose of this dare is to create a clear vision of the legacy toward which you are working with your school family. You may choose to do this activity alone or with others. The choice is yours! You will work on this dare in two phases. First, you'll be listing those things that you want to eliminate from your life (inside and outside of school). Second, you'll be writing down a glimpse of what this future legacy looks like. Finally, you'll be actually creating an outward symbol of this legacy toward which you are working.

Phase One

(Eliminate)

List the things that you have, are, or do in your life that you feel should be eliminated.

Phase Two

(Envision)

Imagine a day in the future where your (or your school family's) legacy for your school has come to fruition. What does this future day in the life of your school look like?

The Dare

For this final phase of the dare, and as the culminating activity for this workbook, you will create an outward symbol of the legacy toward which you are working. Utilizing the answers you provided in the Reflection Questions, Deeper Questions, and the first two phases of this dare in this chapter, perform the following tasks:

1. Gather magazine clippings and prints of online images that match those things that you wish to have, be, and do within your legacy for your school.

2. Create a poster-board collage utilizing these images.

3. Take a photograph of this collage. Send it to us via social media by visiting our website (www.WorldsGreatestHighSchool.com).

4. Place the collage behind your desk in a prominent location that you will see each day.

5. Each morning, let this collage be a reminder of some of the reasons you are working each day to be one step better than the day before – your World's Greatest Me.

Consider repeating this dare, working with a representative group of school family members. Rather than creating a single collage as the final product, create a mural on the side of a prominent building on your campus.

Want to go deeper? Want to further impact your instruction, students, and school? Visit our website and sign up for more free training:

www.WorldsGreatestHighSchool.com

Appendixes

Some Helpful Stuff

Staff Introduction Letter

"Building the World's Greatest High School" Mini-Poster / Flyer

Supplementary Reading Parent Permission Letter

"Building the World's Greatest High School" One-Sheet Synopsis

Please use these appendixes as "guides" in creating your own materials, rather than copying ours. Please do not photocopy or electronically distribute any portion of this book.

Staff Introduction Letter

Dear Family,

As we walk into this new season, I want to take a moment to present to you a framework for impacting teaching and learning that has greatly inspired me over the past months. This framework is called The World's Greatest High School. It comes from a book called *Building the World's Greatest High School*, written by Richard Parkhouse and Dr. Guy E. White. Mr. Parkhouse is an internationally recognized expert on school culture. Dr. White is a current classroom teacher in California who has written a number of books about teaching and teacher leadership. They present some key ideas in their book that I think are definitely worth discussing. Some of these "World's Greatest Values" include:

Value # 1 – We are what we believe – what we believe unifies us.

Value #2 – All students have futures.

Value #3 – No one gets anywhere without a teacher.

Value #4 – All students are gifted and talented.

Value #5 – Every day is an opportunity to become the World's Greatest Me.

Value #6 – Everything we do, we do with PRIDE.

Simply reading through these values, you may have raised an eyebrow or two!

We have purchased the book *Building the World's Greatest High School* for the entire staff, and we have placed one in your box. We ask that you take a moment to read chapters 1-3 over the next ten days in preparation for our January 10 staff meeting.

I look forward to discussing your ideas, disagreements, and inspiration.

Thank you,

My name and signature.

Please use this as a "guide" in creating your own letter, rather than copying ours. Your school has its own unique character that should be appreciated and acknowledged in your letter.

Building the World's Greatest High School

Richard Parkhouse & Dr. Guy E. White

The World's Greatest High School is a place where everyone is becoming the best versions of themselves each day.

The World's Greatest Values

Value # 1

We are what we believe – what we believe unifies us.

Value #2

All students have futures.

Value #3

No one gets anywhere without a teacher.

Value #4

All students are gifted and talented.

Value #5

Every day is an opportunity to become the World's Greatest Me.

Value #6

Everything we do, we do with PRIDE.

www.WorldsGreatestHighSchool.com

Supplementary Reading Parent Permission Letter

Dear Parent/Guardian of _____,

This is _____, your student's leadership teacher/advisor. As our student leaders step into this new semester, I want to take a moment to present to you a framework for impacting teaching and learning that has greatly inspired me over the past months. This framework is called The World's Greatest High School. It comes from a book called *Building the World's Greatest High School (ISBN 978-0984089529)*, written by Richard Parkhouse and Dr. Guy E. White. Mr. is an internationally recognized expert on school culture. Dr. White is a current classroom teacher in California who has written a number of books about teaching and teacher leadership. They present some key ideas in their book that I think are definitely worth discussing. Some of these "World's Greatest Values" include:

Value # 1 – We are what we believe – what we believe unifies us.

Value #2 – All students have futures.

Value #3 – No one gets anywhere without a teacher.

Value #4 – All students are gifted and talented.

Value #5 – Every day is an opportunity to become the World's Greatest Me.

Value #6 – Everything we do, we do with PRIDE.

Simply reading through these values, you may have raised an eyebrow or two!

We have purchased the book *Building the World's Greatest High School* for the purpose of reading excerpts to our student leadership class. However, because this book has not been approved as part of the Master Reading List for our school district, <u>we need your permission for your student to read this book</u>. Our principal has already approved this book to be used, as long as you provide permission. Thank you for your consideration!

☐ <u>Yes</u>, I give permission for my student to read the book.
☐ No, I want my student to have an alternative assignment.

_____
Signature   Date

Please use this as a "guide" in creating your own permission letter, rather than copying ours. Your school and school district has its own unique requirements/laws/procedures that need to be followed.

Building the World's Greatest High School

Richard Parkhouse & Dr. Guy E. White

The World's Greatest High School is a place where everyone is becoming the best versions of themselves each day. The staffulty, parents, students, and community partners of the World's Greatest High School hold six values about teaching and learning.

The World's Greatest Values

Value # 1 - We are what we believe – what we believe unifies us.

What we collectively believe greatly impacts teaching and learning on our campus.

Value #2 - All students have futures.

Every student has a future and educators have the ability to impact that future.

Value #3 - No one gets anywhere without a teacher.

A teacher's impact upon a student's life is exponential and impacts many others.

Value #4 - All students are gifted and talented.

Everyone brings gifts, talents, and skills into the school.

Value #5 - Every day is an opportunity to become the World's Greatest Me.

Each person can become his or her World's Greatest by striving daily to become a better "me" than the day before.

Value #6- Everything we do, we do with PRIDE.

At the World's Greatest High School, the school's one-of-a-kind culture of "Greatness" is clear in everything it does.

www.WorldsGreatestHighSchool.com

Glossary

Academic Rally: A campus-wide celebration where the gifts, talents, and skills of all are intentionally put on display. Staffulty, students, parents, alumni, and community business partners are honored for their roles in helping others become the World's Greatest Me. Inspirational stories of the growth and the role of Mentors in these stories are tangibly illustrated.

Expectations: The anticipated futures that we hold for our peers, our students, and ourselves.

Mediocre High School: A loosely held-together school community that is "okay being okay." People at this school are not challenging themselves or each other to be better than the day before, or their way of challenging one another is inconsistent or ineffective.

Mentors: Those persons who advocate and assist another person in becoming his or her World's Greatest Me.

No Hope High School: A fractured school community that feels that kids don't care, which in turn translates to the kids feeling that their school doesn't care, creating a place where largely no one cares. People at this school say, "You don't understand our kids," "you don't know their challenges," and "they can't learn."

Plans, Planning: The steps that we set to fulfill the expectations that we hold for ourselves, our students, our peers, our school, etc.

Relationships: The means by which the value system of the school is transmitted from one person to another.

Royal Family: The typically recognized sub-set of students, community members, and staffulty at any school. These include, but are not limited to, popular athletic teams such as football and basketball or the players therein; straight-A, perfect attendance, and honor roll students; and homecoming and prom kings and queens. All schools have a Royal Family that is made up of people who are nearly always celebrated and/or put on display as success at school. The Royal Family represents a minority of the school population, such as the academic or athletic percent.

World's Greatest High School: A school community that has collectively agreed to take up and live out the World's Greatest Values.

World's Greatest Me: A person who is intentionally, consistently developing him or herself to become better than the person he or she was the day before.

World's Greatest Values: The six core beliefs of the World's Greatest High School community.

About the Authors

Richard Parkhouse

"Every day is an opportunity to Change Lives and Impact Futures."

Known throughout educational circles as "Park," he brings a wealth of knowledge regarding the transformation of school cultures and increasing school-wide expectations. Park has dedicated himself to developing outstanding student activity and leadership programs nationally. He has been the keynote speaker at the CADA State Convention. He has also spoken at CADA Student Leadership Conferences, ACSA conferences, Jostens® Renaissance® National Conferences, and at the National Association of Student Councils Conference. Park is an active member of the California Association of Activities Directors (CADA) and has written articles for the NASSP *Student Leadership* Magazine. Park's efforts have received national recognition as Park was the recipient of an Earl Reum Award, which recognizes those who mentor the trainers of student leaders. He is a member of the CADA Hall of Fame and was selected for his ability to instill a vision of school-wide excellence for all. As a national presenter for Jostens® Renaissance®, Park was inducted into the

National Jostens® Renaissance® Hall of Fame in the first inaugural class in 1998. This honor was due to his commitment to helping develop Jostens® Renaissance® schools nationally, as well as being the founder of the Academic Pep Rally. He has served as an educator for twenty-five years as a science teacher, coach, activities director, and assistant principal.

During the past eleven years, Park has been working with over 1500 schools as an educator consultant with Jostens, Inc. His forte is the development of positive and interactive school climates. His work includes the development and implementation of bringing the core values of the schools alive, connectedness of students and staff, increasing the role of student leaders on campus, addressing the recognition gap on campus, and focusing on incorporating the core values of teaching and learning into the daily rituals of the school culture. Park's vision is to assist schools in taking their mission statement from artwork on the wall to where you can see it and feel it as you walk the halls. He is a master of creating environments where acknowledgement and recognition is deserved, specific, and meaningful for all stakeholders.

Park presents a wide variety of strategies that have proven to have a lasting effect on schools. These initiatives will bring information and knowledge, but more importantly, staff and students will be involved in the process of enhancing the school climate and effectiveness. The key to the success of his techniques is to create ownership for the stakeholders of the school. This in turn will help to keep the vision and philosophies at the forefront for years to come.

Jostens® and Renaissance® are registered trademarks of Jostens, Inc. and used herein with permission.

About the Authors

Guy E. White, Ed.D.

www.exitingthebakesale.com

Dr. Guy E. White is the founder of Exiting the Bakesale®, the revolutionary fundraising system for schools wanting to raise money without selling wrapping paper and cookie dough. Guy's books, videos, products, online trainings, coaching, and appearances inspire those he serves throughout the world. For these works, those he serves recognize him as providing life-shifting, in-depth development programs for educators.

Guy is a National Board Certified Teacher®, holding the highest level of teacher certification available in the United States. He is a Certified Integral Master Coach™ by Integral Coaching Canada. Guy has "gold standard" accreditations in the teaching and coaching fields respectively.

Guy has contributed to *Leadership in Student Activities* magazine, published by the National Association of Secondary School Principals for members of the National

Association of Student Councils, the National Honor Society, and the National Junior Honor Society. His research, carried in multiple online research databases, on activities directors of highly successful secondary schools is one of the most recent and comprehensive bodies of research on high school co-curricular activities programs in the world.

Meet him and receive more free training at **www.exitingthebakesale.com**

Integral Coach™ and Integral Master Coach™ are registered trademarks in Canada owned by Integral Coaching Canada Inc. and licensed to Guy E. White.

National Board Certified Teacher® is a registered trademark of the National Board for Professional Teaching Standards and is used herein with permission.

Meet the authors and get more free training at

www.worldsgreatesthighschool.com

Made in the USA
Charleston, SC
05 December 2013